THE MOORS MURDERS

IAN BRADY AND MYRA HINDLEY

(Book 3 British Criminals)

by Alan R. Warren

Copyrights

THE MOORS MURDERERS
IAN BRADY AND MYRA HINDLEY

(Book 3 British Criminals)

by Alan R. Warren

Published by
RJ Parker Publishing
March 2019

ISBN 978-1987902600

ENTER TO WIN

Monthly KINDLE HD FIRE Giveaway

***

Drawing each month on the 30th...

***

Enter to WIN
(No Purchase Necessary)

Click HERE   *http://www.rjparkerpublish-*
ing.com/Win-a-Kindle.html

Table of Contents

BOOK DESCRIPTION

It was in Manchester, England in 1965, when the police were called to a possible crime scene at the residence of Ian Brady and girlfriend Myra Hindley. What they found in the upstairs spare bedroom were the remains of 17-year-old Edward Evans, who had been cut into pieces with an axe.

After an investigation and search, the police found two suitcases that were full of graphic pictures and a videotape of a young 10-year-old girl, Lesley Ann Downey who had been missing for months. The pictures showed Leslie tied up and tortured. The tape recorded the assault, and when heard at the police station, made people cry and some even vomit.

The mysteries about to unfold shocked not only the UK, but also the entire world. Soon they would become known as the **'Moors Murders'** – one of the most infamous serial murder cases to come out of Britain.

This book by journalist Alan R. Warren not only reviews the real facts and evidence, describes what REALLY happened behind the closed doors of Brady and Hindley, but also includes actual letters from Ian Brady from the last few years of his life. These give us a unique insight into the mind of Brady; his loves, his hates, and his beliefs in the world of today!

After reviewing several documentaries and reading many of the books already published, I realized that there were many things left unsaid about this case. Even though Myra claimed innocence by not being there when the rapes and murders happened, I suggest that not only was she there, but she was intimately involved; in both the murders and the rapes.

ACKNOWLEDGEMENTS

There are many aspects to writing a true crime book. Not only is there conducting research, reviewing police records, analyzing court documents, reading as many news articles as you can find, traveling to meet and talk to as many people as possible that were involved in the crime, but there is also a considerable attempt made to gain an overall understanding of both the criminals, the victims, and their families.

It is with these things in mind that I am in great appreciation of and want to thank each of the following people by giving them a place in this book:

CODY LACHEY

Cody was a pen pal for both Ian Brady and Myra Hindley, and it is with his help and offer of reading these letters that Cody helped with this book. Cody was an ex-convict who had been in prison in the UK three times: once

8

in the notorious HMP Manchester known as the Notorious Strangeways, and twice in Salford's Forest Bank Prison. Cody had been involved in the criminal underworld as a drug dealer. The 35-year-old, 6'4" man had been shot at and stabbed several times before serving his time in prison.

Cody is now reformed and living in Manchester, England, where he has become a crime commentator covering all aspects of his own personal history of living the life of crime and being in prisons. He has been on several documentaries, spoken to criminology students, and given in depth perspectives on prison reform in the UK.

"It was from my childhood that I went on to be involved with all the lifestyle," Cody told me. "My early lifestyle is also what started me on writing to serial killers who were in prison. I really enjoyed discussing the cases with the killers and wanted to hear their story."

JACKIE DENNISON

Jackie Dennison has been in my life for quite a few years now. I first saw her on the television series 'Rescue Mediums'. In that series, Jackie worked as a psychic medium. With a partner, she would go to haunted houses and help the spirit that was causing some sort of distress to the home owner cross over and leave the home in peace.

I have worked for several radio shows on many radio stations so far in my life, sometimes as host and sometimes as a producer. It was when I was producing the 'Julie Sav Show', a medium living and working in the UK, that I first booked Jackie to be on the show. We had a great time and clicked instantly.

Years later, while researching for this book, I was reviewing a documentary on the Moors murders from the UK. It was during that documentary where I saw Jackie discussing Winnie Johnson and the loss of her son, Keith Bennett...one of the victims of Ian Brady and Myra Hindley. So, I reached out to Jackie immediately and asked about her personal feelings on the case...not only a medium but as a friend of the family.

This is a very important aspect to this book. At the time of its' writing, all of the murderers, victims, and even their families, such as Winnie Johnson, have since passed on. In order to accurately complete the writing of a book that gives you the facts and describes the intimate details of the crimes, it must include the personal touch or testimony of someone close to the victims. They are the only ones who can express the feelings and effects of that crime to that level of detail.

A DEDICATION TO ALL WHO WERE LOST

JOHN KILBRIDE, LESLEY ANN-DOWNEY, EDWARD EVANS, PAULINE READE, AND KEITH BENNETT

FOREWARD

I was a child when the horrific story of the Moors Murders began to unfold, and I remember the shock and disbelief that a woman could lure children knowing that they would be murdered! Parents became over cautious, continuously telling their children not to stray far from the house and not to talk to strangers. The trust was broken, and the world would never be quite the same again. Those heinous acts would haunt me from that day.

Thirty years later the body of Pauline Reade was found, and we all hoped and prayed that Keith Bennett would be found too, but to this day that has never happened.

Some years later I met Keith's Mum, Winnie Johnson, myself and my sister in law were invited into her home. Winnie gave me an envelope to hold. On looking inside, I saw a pair of child's glasses, Keith's glasses. As I held them in my hand, I was overwhelmed by the enormity of it all. "Its all I have left" she said, and I was overcome by emotion. From that moment Winnie became part of my life. She lived about an hour drive away and at least twice a month we would go and pick her up and take her to the Moors where she loved to be. She said although this was the place where Keith had been murdered, it helped her to feel close to him. As the years rolled by, I would pick Winnie up and bring her to my own home or to my parents' home, who welcomed her with open arms. She loved my Mums Sunday dinners, good old-fashioned cooking she said. We would go for days out to museums or day trip to the seaside. She was a tough cookie and could swear like a trooper. I knew that if she was calling me names it was because she liked me; it was her way of endearment.

For all the joviality, Winnie never stopped grieving for her son, nor did she stop searching. She could cry within a heartbeat when thinking or talking about him. The tears were genuine and came from a place deep within her soul. It was as painful to her in that moment as it had been the day he went missing. Winnie went to her grave never knowing where her son lay on the Moors.

I was with Winnie on the afternoon before she passed away in the Hospice. I took her a small rose bush, her favourite flower. Her garden was full of them, they reminded her of Keith. We would take flowers to the Moors every anniversary of the day he went missing and a wreath of flowers at Christmas. I kissed her goodbye and told her I loved her. She died later that night. For Winnie the search is over, and I believe that she is reunited with Keith once more. I pray that someday his body will be found so that his family can honour him in the way that his Mother always wanted him to be honoured, and in Winnies words "he can be brought back home to the people of Manchester".

Jackie Dennison

INTRODUCTION – THE LOST SOUL

It was the morning of Friday, March 5, 2010. Winnie Johnson was awakened by what sounded like a voice calling out to her. She had sat down the night before on her sofa, thinking about the memorial service that was finally going to happen 46 years after her son, Keith Bennett, had disappeared.

She soon realized that the sounds she was hearing were short gusts of wind blasting across her roof, and not anybody calling to her. As she sat up slowly, she could see that it was still very dark out. She walked towards her living room window and opened her curtains, noticing that it was very cloudy.

It had been a bitterly cold winter with plenty of snow. The news reported that it was the worst winter Manchester had seen since 1987. She wrapped her robe around herself and tied the rope tightly, as it had been disheveled sometime during her night on the sofa.

Winnie walked over to the fireplace mantle and picked up the picture of her son. Walking back to the sofa, she focused on Keith's eyes in the picture. She was trying to connect with him, trying to get answers, as she had done for so many years.

Sitting back down, Winnie quietly said "Look at my eyes, they are tired and have no answers. They don't know much, but they know that I love you, and I guess that's all they're going to know."

She sighed and placed the picture on the coffee table. Winnie willed herself not to cry. She had cried too many times already, and no matter how hard she cried, no matter if she screamed and yelled even, nothing would change.

Winnie replayed in her head the last time she saw her son. She was walking to the market and her son was running off to meet up with his friends to go see a movie. She remembered waving at him and smiling. Every time she rewound and relived this in her mind, she wanted to change it. She even tried to change it. She desperately told him, "No, you cannot go, you are to stay her with me and help me do my shopping." But even in her she re-imagined scenario of Keith coming to the market with her, he would somehow disappear from the store, and she would end up in the same place - Keith was gone.

Just before 11 a.m. that same day, Councilor Jim McArdle helped Winnie into the memorial service for Keith at the Manchester Cathedral. Her hair was combed flat across her head, tied back with a band keeping it out of her face, and she wore a black and white speckled dress with a long magenta sweater over it.

Winnie stood in front of a large crowd of people, made up of her family, friends and neighbors, and the room went silent. She was trembling and felt dizzy. It was all very overwhelming. Not only was this the memorial service that she had always prayed for her son to celebrate his life, it was also the last step in closing the criminal case of his murder. Winnie reached out her right arm and held onto the stand that was dedicated to her son, and held on tightly, as to help keep her balance as she spoke.

Winnie spoke to the crowd. She expressed the love that she had for her son, and that she believed he was with her to this day, watching over them, and he was in the church now. She went on to thank everyone for being there, not only at the service, but with her through her journey to find her lost son, or as she called him, her 'lost soul.'

After the memorial, Winnie was off to the Saddleworth Moors to the spot that was identified by Ian Brady, Keith's murderer, as Keith's resting place. When she arrived, there was a small group of people assembled. It was a large, beautiful grassy field with a wood post barbed wire fence running beside the road they traveled to get there. The people had all brought tokens of love and sorrow, such as flowers, teddy bears, and some pictures of Keith, and tied them to the posts of the fence.

Winnie now stood in the same spot she had stood in years before, when she came dressed in work clothes with a shovel to dig in search of her son's remains. Even though, Ian Brady had decided to help detectives find the remains of two of his murder victims, one being Keith Bennett, they had no success in finding Keith's body that day. In fact, they still have not found him today.

As his grieving mother dubbed him, Keith Bennett is now known as the 'Lost Soul'.

WINNIE JOHNSON DIGGING IN THE MOORS FOR HER SON'S REMAINS

CHAPTER 1 - ALL I EVER KNEW WAS YOU

IAN BRADY AND MYRA HINDLEY AT THE MOORS

IAN BRADY

Ian Duncan Stewart was born on Sunday, January 2, 1938 in Glasgow, Scotland. Ian's mother, Maggie Stewart, was an unmarried waitress who struggled to pay her bills. The struggle became too much and when Ian was just two months old, so she gave him over to her neighbors, the Sloan family, to raise. The Sloan family was an average middle-class family with four children who lived close enough to Maggie that she could still keep in contact with her son.

Regarding his birthdate, later in life, Ian Brady told a journalist he "loathed the first day of each week", since by Scottish law, Sundays were closed to prevent any prospect of merriment. "Sunday was not the day to be born on, especially not this Sunday, and I found myself illegitimate before taking my first breath. In my case, of course, most people would prefer the term bastard."

Ian started to develop a dark side to his behavior when he was about four years old. It is reported that he began his descent into darkness by torturing small animals. He broke one dog's leg, set another dog on fire and even decapitated a cat.

When Ian was nine years old, the Sloan's moved to the suburbs of Glasgow, so he no longer had easy access to his mother. After they settled into their new home, Ian started to attend the Shadowlands Academy for gifted children, and everything seemed to be going well for him at first.

Ian's early violent behavior continued in their new home. In fact, it worsened. Instead of him inflicting violence on animals, he would now torture younger neighborhood kids. Eventually, Ian started to break into people's homes and steal things. He was caught when he was 15 years old and ended up in juvenile court. Ian then decided to quit school and work any job he could get. He worked as a tea boy at a shipyard once, and then as a messenger for a butcher.

Everything came to a sudden halt when Ian's violent tendencies boiled over. He was arrested for using a switchblade knife on his girlfriend after he discovered she went to a dance with another boy. After this, Ian was put on probation, and sent back to his mother's house to live by the court. Ian's mother was now living in Manchester and married to an Irish man named Patrick Brady.

Patrick was a fruit seller at the Smithfield Market, and he hired Ian as a fruit porter. Within a few months, however, Ian was caught stealing a bag of lead seals from the store and was fired and arrested. At the time, Ian was only 17, so he was sentenced to two years in a British youth prison in Hatfield…a prison that was designed to help reform young offenders rather than to punish them.

In keeping with what was becoming normal behavior for Ian, he got into trouble at the youth prison as well. There, he was found to be brewing his own alcohol. He was then sent to a different young offender prison, designed with punishment in mind, in Hull.

On November 14, 1957, Ian was released and returned to his home in Manchester. Next he started a new job and started studying to be an accountant. It wasn't long before he started working as a clerk at Millward's Merchandising, a wholesale chemical plant in Gorton, just south of Manchester.

Around this time of his life, Ian started reading about the Nazis. He even taught himself the German language so that he could read Adolf Hitler's "Mein Kampf". Brady was also a huge fan of the work of The Marquis de Sade, who was known for his very vivid accounts of sexual violence.

About three years later, in January 1961, Millward's Merchandising hired a typist by the name of Myra Hindley. Myra was approximately 20 years old at the time, very tall, and had peroxide-blonde hair. Brady never paid much attention to Hindley at first; he thought of her as just another of the female workers. He never liked her hairstyle, and she had heat marks on her legs from sitting too close to her fireplace at her home. Myra worked in a small room next to Brady, took dictation, and typed his letters.

Myra, on the other hand, was far more attracted to Brady, as she admitted in her diary. She would write things like 'Ian looked at me today' or 'I wonder if Ian is courting. Still feel the same', and 'I love Ian all over again. He has a cold and I would love to mother him.'

On December 23, Millward's had their annual Christmas party. The staff would spend a few hours at a nearby pub and afterward all return to the mill for some drinks. When they returned, quite a few of the typists were dancing and drinking in the office. Brady joined them. He gave them all a Christmas kiss, and when Myra walked in the room, Brady kissed her as well. It all started as easy as that.

Myra and Brady made plans to meet later that night at a different pub. After a couple of drinks, he took her to see the movie 'King of Kings', which was a biblical movie. In the coming weeks, Brady would take Myra out to see several movies, and they would stay up all night discussing topics such as religion, and the Nazis of Germany.

MYRA HINDLEY

Like Ian, Myra came from a broken family as well. Her father was an alcoholic and would constantly beat her. He was such a strict disciplinarian that when a boy pushed her down and scratched her at eight years old, he demanded that she go find the boy and knock him out.

At first, Myra was hesitant to go find the boy, but her father told her that if she didn't, he would beat her until she was knocked out. So she searched for the boy, and when she found him, she fought him until she knocked him out. To Myra's father, she scored her first victory.

Myra carried a great deal of guilt with her over the death of a friend. In 1957, she was asked to go swimming in a reservoir with her best friend at the time, but she refused. When the boy ended up drowning, she blamed herself.

When Myra and Ian met, the couple connected immediately. They both had the same tastes and desires. Upon Ian's urging, Myra learned to speak German as well. He thought the two of them would be able to speak covertly in public without anybody else knowing what they were saying. After watching X-rated films, they would go back to Brady's home, read to each other in German, and drink German wine. Their fascination with "all-things-German" even persuaded Myra to color her hair blonde to look more Aryan. She also started to wear red lipsticks, high boots, short skirts, and leather jackets.

The couple had also created code words and gestures for body movements, such as saying the word 'Groucho' and rising your eyebrows twice would mean to follow the direction of my eyes.

When either of them spotted a sexually attractive man or woman, they would say 'DC', which stood for delicious creature.

Though at work, the couple kept their distance from each other. They didn't want to let on to the other employees that they were now romantically involved with each other.

In the early part of 1962, Ian and Myra discovered Saddleworth Moor, which is 1600 feet above sea level and 24 miles wide. It occupies 400 square miles of land located between Manchester and Huddersfield. According to Brady's letters, it was pure serendipity that they found the moor. Brady claimed that in the summer he would quite often skip out of work and take his motorbike out for a ride. On one of those mornings, he ended up on Saddleworth Moor.

Much later, in 1979, Myra wrote to the British Home Secretary, "Within months he had convinced me that there was no God at all. He could have told me that the earth was flat, the moon was made of green cheese and the sun rose in the west, I would have believed him, such was his power of persuasion."

In early 1963, the couple began to make plans to rob banks and Myra joined a gun club. She would now be able to buy guns. Ian had been convicted of crimes in the past, so he was not allowed to own a gun. Hindley also rented a van, and the couple drove around to different banks devising plans of how and when they would rob certain banks. The van was large enough to hold their weapons and carry the money from the robberies.

Around this time, Brady also became very interested in photography and created his own dark room at the home and began taking nude photos of Hindley.

Maureen Hindley, Myra's younger sister, had a boyfriend, David Smith. She knew that Brady had his own expensive photography equipment and dark room, so Maureen asked if he could take some pictures of her to give to David. While Brady was taking the photos of Maureen, he asked her questions about David. Ian wanted to find out if David was looking to make some money.

MAUREEN HINDLEY AND DAVID SMITH

During this question period, Maureen told Brady that her new boyfriend had been seen with Myra's neighbor, Pauline Reade, and he was still playing the field. David also had trouble with the Hindley family as it was reported that when he was hanging around waiting for Maureen, her mother would send him away saying, "I can't stand the thought of Mo having anything to do with that dirty bugger."

Myra and Brady decided to find out who this David Smith was and went looking for him. The first time they saw him he was standing in an entranceway to an alley, with his back leaning against the wall. Smith was wearing drainpipe jeans and jacket. Brady said he thought Smith didn't look promising at all, and in fact, wished he went with his first impression of Smith, as he would still be a free man today.

Brady suggested to Myra that a blood related-accomplice would be a safeguard against him talking to the police about their crimes. Myra wanted to make sure that Maureen would never be involved in any of the criminal activities Brady told her that if they didn't use Smith and the couple didn't get married, they could take care of him, which made Myra smile..

David Smith would marry Maureen though when they found out that she was pregnant. It was less than a year from their meeting. Maureen's family didn't accept the match. Smith didn't have a good job and had an awful record with the police. He was also a year and a half younger than Maureen was.

David's mother, Joyce Hull, abandoned him when he was only 2 years old. His father, Jack Smith, a travelling maintenance fitter, was rarely home with his son. It would be Jack Smith's parents, Annie and John Smith, who would take care of David and eventually adopt him. They lived in Ardwick, Manchester.

David became a juvenile delinquent who would fight with his grandfather so much that they sent him to the Rose Hill Remand Home. After his release from that home, he moved to the Stanley Grove School, where he became a boxer and won a boxing championship. That would only last a short time before Smith punched the headmaster of the school, Mr. Silver, in a fight over wearing his school uniform correctly. Smith wanted tight pants, almost skin tight, and altered them himself. David was expelled.

Jack's father eventually returned and decided to take a job in Manchester. He took David with him to live at #13 Wiles Street in

Gorton, which was just around the corner from Myra's house and next door to Pauline Reade.

Smith joined the All Saints School in Gorton after he got settled in with his father. Unfortunately, David used his cricket bat to break the fingers of another student who called him a bastard. He was charged with assault with wounding. He was only 11.

When he turned 15, he broke into a house and was caught. He appeared before the magistrate, who sentenced him to three years of probation.

In October 1963 (three months after the murder of Pauline Reade), Brady met David Smith in person for the first time. Smith was waiting outside of Millward's for Maureen to finish for the day; and when Brady saw him, he offered Smith a ride home.

CHAPTER 2 - PAULINE READE

PAULINE READE

"First things first, we need a written plan." The couple sat on the living room floor and made their plans while they drank warm German wine. By the end of the night, they had created a master list. On that list, Brady had some rules that had to be followed no matter what:

1.	There must be no thread connecting the starting point with the destination.

2.	All surfaces must be free of tire and footmarks, hairs, fibers and fingerprints.

3.	There must be duplicates of all clothing, including shoes. The set used in the day must be burned and the ashes thrown into the river.

4.	Buttons must be carefully counted and cleaned.

5.	The vehicle must be thoroughly cleaned and polished before and after the event.

6.	Both the inner workings and the outer surfaces of guns must be free of fingerprints.

7.	Bullet heads must be scored to turn them into a shapeless mass, destroying all ballistic marking on impact.

8.	Plastic sheets must cover the interior of the vehicle.

9.	False number plates must be used, and the vehicle must be parked where it can be seen from overlooking windows.

10.	All things used as a weapon must be broken up and disposed of over a wide area.

Their house had to be cleared of anything that might be incriminating, and thus collected by the police. They placed these items into suitcases and dropped them off at railway stations. Brady wanted the team to establish alibis that could remain steadfast for 14 days. Anything after that could go to a "vague" status, as most people can't remember what they did last week unless something special was happening.

The master plan was placed into a large envelope along with a contact list, maps of the places they planned to rob, photographs, an address book, and tapes. They then hid the envelope amongst other papers in a locked room at Millward's Merchandising. These were the very documents that Myra destroyed in the first four days that Brady was in prison, while she was still free.

Myra joined the rifle club so that she was able to purchase guns. Brady wanted her to get one rifle, a .45, and a .38 snub nose gun, as he didn't trust automatics.

Brady and Hindley's planned robberies would never happen. Instead, they moved on to something much more personal: rape and murder.

How this change happened is still not known. The purpose of getting a gun license for Hindley was so she could amass weapons in order to rob a bank. The van they rented became a vehicle that would carry a body instead of weapons or the money they would have taken from their planned bank heists.

Next door to Brady and Hindley lived Joan and Amos Reade. Their oldest daughter, Pauline, was 16 years old, and their son, Paul, was 13. Pauline went to the same school as Maureen Hindley and David Smith, and was raised as a catholic. She worked as an apprentice in her father's bakery.

On Friday, July 12, 1963, Pauline was on her way to a local dance at the Railway's Workers' Social Club on Chapman Street, a 10-minute walk from her home. Pauline called two of her friends to ask them to go with her to the dance, but both were not allowed to go because their mothers didn't like that there was going to be alcohol served.

It was about 7:45 p.m. when Pauline finished getting ready and left for the dance. She wore a black blouse, a pink and gold shirt, a knitted cardigan, a blue coat, and a pair of white stiletto heels. As Pauline walked down Gorton Lane, she was enjoying the warm evening sun on her face, which also partially blinded her from seeing anything in front of her.

As she walked beside a parked black van, she could hear the driver's side window squeak as it rolled down. Myra called out to Pauline and asked her where she was going. In reply, Pauline stopped and told her about the dance. She recognized Myra, and so Pauline relaxed into a conversation about school and friends they had in common.

Myra pointed at some 78-rpm records (The popular medium for music at this time) that were sitting on the passenger seat of her van. She offered to give them to Pauline if she would go to Saddleworth Moor and help her find an expensive glove she lost when she was out there earlier that morning.

Pauline was early for the dance, so she thought that she could fill the spare time helping Myra find the glove. She collected the records and placed them on her lap and got into the van. And the two of them headed for the moor.

Meanwhile, Ian Brady was at his home with his parents, creating an alibi. He deliberately asked them the time before he left, so if they were ever asked, they would remember when he was there. When Brady got to the place on Gorton Lane where Myra should have been, he saw that the van was gone. He knew that she must have found a victim. He headed for the moor.

Brady arrived at the moor and parked his bike beside Myra's van. He still wasn't sure who the victim was going to be. Would it be a boy or girl? He lifted the goggles off his face, removed his gloves and walked towards Myra and Pauline. They were both sitting in the van having a smoke. He walked over, squeezed in beside Myra and lit a cigarette for himself.

After Myra introduced Brady to Pauline, she told them that they had better start searching for her lost glove before it got too dark. They put out their cigarettes and headed out into the moor, with Brady walking about 15 feet in front of the girls. Everything was normal and not out of the ordinary, as they were still in view of cars that were travelling by. They slowly made it over a small hill and out of sight of the road, when Myra gave Brady the signal, "Groucho'. Brady walked up behind Pauline and grabbed her head putting her in a strangle hold.

Pauline fell to the ground and stared into Brady's eyes in shock. Brady told her to stay quiet and she would be all right. She turned to Myra, but instead of getting any help, Myra just smiled and told Pauline to keep quiet.

Pauline then shouted out that she was unwell, which meant that it was that time of the month for her. Myra got down on her knees beside Pauline and started to unbutton her coat. Brady stood up and kept watch over the moor while Myra finished undressing Pauline.

Myra then started to fondle Pauline's breasts. Pauline lay down and was submissive, letting Myra now kiss her breasts. After Myra completely stripped Pauline down, Brady undressed and joined in having sex with Pauline.

The sun had gone down behind the mountains and it was getting dark now. Brady stood up and told Pauline to get dressed. She started to put her clothes back on and when she reached for her necklace, Myra grabbed it from her and told her "you won't need this where you're going!" This made Brady mad enough to slap Myra across the face, and she went silent.

Brady went back to the van to get what he needed to finish the job and left the girls by themselves. While he was gone, Myra picked up a knife she had brought and attempted to stab Pauline in the chest. The knife didn't penetrate since the blade was bent. So Myra punched Pauline in the face a few times causing Pauline's nose to bleed.

When Brady returned and saw that Myra had not killed Pauline yet, he took his own knife and cut her throat. Blood gushed out of Pauline's neck, but she was still alive, so Brady slashed her neck again. This time it severed the carotid artery, and she was dead in seconds.

Myra told Brady that the girl they had just killed was Pauline Reade. At first Brady didn't remember who she was. Then he remembered his conversation with Myra's sister, Maureen, and realized that they had just eliminated her competition for David Smith.

It was now too dark to take pictures as keepsakes of Pauline, so Ian told Myra to take the knife and camera back to the van and get the spade. When she returned, Brady dug into the soft peat of the moor about five feet. He grabbed Pauline by her shoulders while Myra held her legs, and they dropped her into the hole.

Brady shovelled peat on top of Pauline's body until she was fully buried, and Myra pulled up handfuls of grass by the roots and stomped them over top of the grave to make sure that there was no sign of a disturbance. The couple counted how many steps it took to get back to the van so that they could find the grave again if they ever had to.

The couple changed out of all the clothes they were wearing during the rape and murder, and Myra headed back home with them in her van. Brady stayed at the moor and buried the spade he had used to bury Pauline's body.

When Myra pulled up and parked her van in front of their home, she noticed Pauline Reade's mother out searching the street for her daughter. By the time Brady got back home, there was nobody on the street looking for Pauline.

It was now 2:30 in the morning. Ian and Myra were cutting up the clothes that they wore during their crime and burning them. Meanwhile, Pauline's father got out of bed and went to the social club to look for his daughter.

Myra had quite a different recollection of what happened that night at the moor with Pauline Reade. She claimed that she was waiting on Gorton Lane and when Pauline got close to the van, Brady, who was parked and sitting on his motorbike across the street, flashed his headlights. This was the signal for her that he chose who he wanted, and she was to get that person.

Myra claimed that she drove Pauline to the moor, and Brady followed them there. When they parked, Brady and Pauline went looking for the glove alone, and they were gone for about one hour. Brady returned alone and took her out to where Pauline was already dead. He told her to stay with the body while he went and got the spade to bury her.

It was then that Myra figured that Brady had raped Pauline as well, since Pauline's clothes were all dishevelled. Myra claimed that after this she became scared for her life, and her family, as she could no longer trust what Brady was going to do.

Several weeks passed, and the police still had no leads on the missing Pauline Reade. Brady and Myra soon got over the panic and excitement of committing the murder, and moved on to their next victim.

Around this time, Myra was in a minor traffic accident and ended up becoming friends with the policeman who wrote her a citation. Myra claims that she eventually fell in love with this police officer, who would come over to her house and leave out the back when they heard Brady's motorbike approaching.

In Myra's later version, she claimed that she met the policeman when he came to look at her van, which she had decided to sell. Brady claims that he encouraged the affair between Myra and the policeman so that they would be privy to inside information. It should be said that the policeman came forward after Myra was arrested and was cleared of any involvement in the murders.

A couple of months later, Brady and Myra decided it would be safe to head back to the moor and return to their normal routine of drinking and hanging out there. They were in shock when they arrived to see that North Sea Gas had been digging a trench for a new pipeline and narrowly missed their hidden spade that was buried in a shallow grave there. Even more terrifying to the couple was just how close it was to where they buried Pauline Reade, who lay buried just a few yards away.

The couple spent the day at Saddleworth taking pictures of Myra and her dog, Puppet, on and around Pauline's grave.

On their ride home something happened that resonated with Brady for years to come. As they turned a sharp corner coming out of the moor and Brady was flooring the bike, he saw a young girl strolling across the road. She was walking so lightly that it was like she was floating. Abruptly, Brady slammed on the brakes and came to a sliding halt. The girl turned and looked at him in the eyes and said, "Sorry, God bless." Then she continued across the road as if nothing happened.

CHAPTER 3 - JOHN KILBRIDE

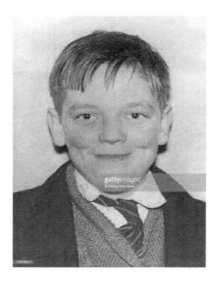

JOHN KILBRIDE

Years before, one of Brady's girlfriends had given him a sealed pack of Tarot cards. In his book 'Gates of Janus', Brady claimed, "I used them from a psychological point of view, not occult. The combination of intricate designs and colors, plus the multi-interpretational relationship of meanings, made the cards not only a meditative but also a psychological conduit, providing a conduit to the subconscious, reflecting inner doubts or confidence in some immediate project at hand. Based on a study of such self-serving amateurs, I do not hesitate to state that one could achieve a higher percentage of success with a pack of Tarot cards."

Autumn arrived softly in Gorton yet it was still mild and dry. The only way you could tell summer was over was the leaves falling from the trees, covering the roads. One night while drinking wine, Brady and Hindley pulled out their master plans, placed a map on the living room table, and started to plot for their next victim.

The couple decided they would go to a different area to pick up their next victim. They didn't want it to be too close to where Pauline went missing and they wanted to avoid being recognized by someone they knew. They soon decided on a town five miles from Gorton, Ashton-Under-Lyne. They grabbed their jackets and decided to go check out the town. When they arrived in their newly selected destination, they came across the Ashton Market. Brady decided that the market was the perfect place to pick someone up because the long dark street running behind the market had no houses on it. They carefully made their plans and decided to make the following Saturday, November 23, the day of their next killing.

Brady rented a car for their trip to Ashton Market; they thought it would be best to change their vehicle every time they were going to pick up a new victim. The couple went to Manchester on Friday, the night before, just in case the police checked to see who had rented cars on the day the person went missing. When they were in the station renting the car, they heard about President Kennedy of the United States being shot. When they arrived home and turned on the television, all programming had been pre-empted, and everything was about the Kennedy assassination and the possibility of World War III starting.

Sheila and Pat Kilbride, John Kilbride's parents, were married, in their 30's, and lived in Ashton-Under-Lyne with their six children, only two miles from the market. John was 12 years old, their oldest child, and had just started to attend a Roman Catholic secondary school.

November 23 started out like every other Saturday morning for the Kilbride family: first, a family breakfast, followed by everyone doing his or her chores for the day. John asked his mother if he could go to the movies with his friend, John Ryan. They went to see the movie 'The Mongols' with Jack Palance.

The movie ended about 4:30 p.m. that afternoon and the boys decided to go to the market to try and make some money. They knew that a lot of the vendors would pay kids to help them pack up their wares after the market closed.

Sometime around 6 p.m., a dark fog had descended over the market and John Ryan decided he wanted to go home. When he left, Kilbride was standing beside a large garbage bin. In order to know what was to follow, we only have two witnesses, Ian and Myra, and their accounts differ. Both versions are included.

.

BRADY'S STORY

According to Brady, everything went as planned. Myra spoke to the boy at the market and told him that she lost her glove while Brady watched the crowd to make sure that nobody was watching the two talking. Myra took Kilbride to her car and they both got in. Myra then picked up Brady at a prearranged place and they headed to the moor.

Brady claims that when they arrived, they parked and the three of them walked into the moor. Kilbride kept asking the couple what they were doing there, and where were they going. He was getting scared because it was getting dark, and he couldn't see well enough by now to find a glove.

Brady gave the 'Groucho' comment and Myra grabbed Kilbride. He started to struggle and kick at her. Brady then joined in and helped bring Kilbride to the ground. Brady pulled Killbride's pants and underwear down, while Myra held the boy's legs. Brady then sexually assaulted him.

After the assault, Brady strangled the boy to death with his bare hands. Brady went to find the spade and returned to dig a grave for Kilbride's body. When the hole was deep enough, the couple dropped him into it face down. Before Brady covered Killbride with dirt, he slapped his backside and shouted out "Take that, you bastard!"

MYRA'S STORY

Myra claimed that she was wearing a black wig that day and waited on a side street while Brady picked up Kilbride. She claims that Brady got him into the car by offering him some sherry for helping him find a lost glove.

They drove to Saddleworth Moor and parked. Myra claimed she stayed in the car while Brady and Kilbride walked down into the moor. While she was waiting in the car, she went into the trunk and took out a rifle that they had placed there earlier that day. She waited another half an hour and flashed her car lights towards the moor. She received three flashes back from a flashlight, and within minutes

Brady returned to the car. He had the spade and one of the boy's shoes in his hands.

Brady told her that he had tried to cut the boys throat with his knife, but it had a serrated blade and was too blunt, so he had to strangle the boy with his shoestring.

One flaw with Myra's version of events is that records show that the rifle she had was bought in 1964, which was after this murder.

Ian Brady also denied Myra's claims of him using a knife; why would he use a short, blunt knife? After all, he was able to almost decapitate Pauline Reade with a knife, and he would have had no problem killing a boy like John Kilbride with a knife as well.

The couple returned home and followed the same routine as they had after Pauline Reade's murder: burning all their clothes and Kilbride's shoe as well, cleaning the car thoroughly and returning it to the auto rental shop.

The Kilbride family called the police the next morning, on Sunday. Any news reports of the now missing boy were over shadowed by the Kennedy assassination, but the locals were still able to find about 100 volunteers to help look for John.

To help with this case, the police used a psychic, Annie Lansley, who had a vision that could help. She saw John Kilbride's resting place on a downward slope, with a skyline completely barren and no trees in sight, with a main road nearby and a stream. Brady's response was that he thought the psychic was quite accurate, but he didn't believe in the psychic stuff. He also commented that if she had been accurate about their next victim, she would have been murdered.

In the months following the murder of John Kilbride, Brady broke one of his own rules and wrote Kilbride's name in his master plan book. Later, this would cause the couple some problems with the police.

CHAPTER 4 - KEITH BENNETT

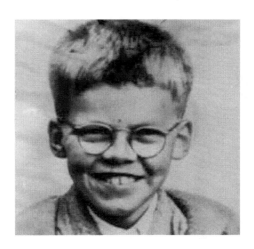

THE 'LOST SOUL' KEITH BENNETT

Keith Bennett was 12-years-old, the oldest of four children, who vanished on June 16, 1964. He lived in Longsight with his stepfather, Jimmy Johnson, and mother Winnie, who was seven months pregnant when Keith disappeared.

Winnie planned to go play bingo on the night of June 16, at 8 p.m. She left the house at 7:45 p.m. and took Keith with her. He was heading to stay with his grandmother for the night, as he did once a week, and the two parted ways at the crossroads. He had just broken his glasses the night before at a swimming competition. Keith was dressed in a t-shirt, blue jeans, a white leather jacket, and black shoes.

Myra Hindley was parked on the street waiting for just the right victim to come along. Once she found them, she would lure them into her vehicle and take them to their death. When she saw Bennett that night in June, she offered him some money if he could help her lift some boxes. Like any young boy wanting a few extra dollars, he eagerly got into the car with her and they drove off.

MYRA'S STORY

Myra claimed that when she picked up Bennett, Brady was in the back seat of the car already. It was Brady who saw Bennett and told her that he was the one. She then drove to the Saddleworth Moor and parked the car.

Myra then claimed that Brady and Bennett walked ahead of her into the moor. She kept a distance behind them on purpose so that she could keep an eye out for anybody that might be around. At one point Brady signalled to Myra to stop following them and to stay where she was.

She stayed in that spot until Brady returned, which was about half an hour later. He was carrying the spade and Bennett wasn't with him. Myra said she asked Brady if he had sex with the boy, and he wouldn't answer her. Myra said that she never did see Bennett's body, and after, the couple walked back to the car and drove home.

Brady developed the pictures he had taken of Keith and Myra said the boy was covered in blood. The pictures were too blurry and didn't please Brady, so he destroyed them.

BRADY'S STORY

According to Brady, after they parked, all three of them walked into the moor. While they were walking, Bennett told the couple that he had to be at his grandmother's within an hour since he was supposed to spend the night with her. Myra assured Bennett that they would get him back in time and not to worry.

Brady knew exactly where they were heading, as the couple had planned this murder as they had the two previous murders. The three of them walked for about three miles before Brady stopped and started to whistle a tune.

This was the signal to Myra to overtake the boy. Bennett started to scream in a panic, and Brady grabbed the boy's neck from behind. Bennett fell onto the ground and started to kick and scream, just like John Kilbride had. While Myra was wrestling with the boy on the ground, Brady jumped on his back and put his hands around his neck. Myra then pulled the boys pants down and held onto his legs while Brady proceeded to sexually assault the boy, keeping his hands around Bennett's neck. After Brady finished, he strangled Bennett with his hands.

Brady stood up and got dressed while Myra turned the boy's body around so that he was lying on his back. Brady grabbed his camera and started to take pictures of Keith. The couple buried Bennett just as they had the two previous murders. This time, Brady marked the grave with a large stone. The two walked back to the car in the dark, drove home and followed the same steps as with the other murders by burning their clothes and cleaning the car thoroughly.

The morning after Keith went missing, his grandmother went to see Winnie to find out why Keith never came to her house for the night. The two women were upset and started looking for Keith, checking his school and the local medical clinic. No one had seen him.

Keith's stepfather became the prime suspect for the police, as they checked under the floor of their house and even dug up their garden. The rumors around the town ran rampant. Neighbors thought Keith had been killed by his stepfather and dumped in the river.

CHAPTER 5 - LESLEY ANN DOWNEY

LESLEY ANN-DOWNEY

Brady and Hindley had murdered three people so far − raped them, killed them, and buried them in the spot that they died. All three murders had been committed outside, but the next murder would be different. It would be committed indoors.

It was August 1964, and Myra's sister Maureen, now 18, had married David Smith, who was 16. Maureen was seven months' pregnant. None of Maureen's family attended the wedding. Brady devised a plan to take Maureen and David out for the day as a honeymoon present. The four of them ended up out at the moor with several bottles of wine.

The women stayed where they parked and talked while the men walked away into the distance and spent several hours together. According to Brady, this was the first time that he brought up the opportunity for Smith to make some money by helping him out.

When the four arrived home, the men stayed downstairs by themselves for hours discussing plans, while the sisters went up to bed. This was the first of many drinking nights the two couples would have. About the same time, Myra, who had been living with her grandmother, moved to a new house, and Brady moved in with them.

One night when the couple was out shopping, they saw an advertisement for a fair happening in the area on Boxing Day, December 26. They were both excited at the fact there would be lots of children coming to the fair. It was time to go home and make plans for another murder.

On December 26 at around 2 p.m., Myra took her grandmother to her son's house across town, and returned to pick her up later that night, around 9:30 p.m.

10-year-old Lesley Ann Downey lived with her mother Ann, and brother Tommy. Ann had been dating a man named Alan West, whom she eventually married. On December 26, the day of the fair, Lesley, Tommy, and a few other friends went to the fair as they had done in the previous years. Lesley was wearing her red dress with lace, a pink sweater, red shoes, and a blue coat. She had six pennies for spending money.

After the kids ran out of money, they headed home. Lesley noticed a show going on, and she wanted to stay and watch it. She told the others to head back, and she would catch up to them.

MYRA'S STORY

Myra claimed that Brady found Lesley and was with the girl first. Brady dropped some boxes beside Lesley and asked if she would help pick them up for some money. The three of them placed the boxes into the car and drove off.

When they arrived at their house, it was Brady who took Lesley upstairs into a bedroom and left Myra alone downstairs. She claims to have kept an eye out for anybody that might come by the house, and that Brady told her to fill the bathtub with warm water. She did what she was told and waited in the bathroom, and when the water in the tub became cold, she drained the tub and filled it up again.

Myra became worried and went into the bedroom. She saw Lesley lying on the bed face down, and she figured that Lesley was dead. Myra saw a lot of blood running down her legs, which made her think that Lesley had been raped.

Like other stories that Hindley told about the previous murders, this story doesn't fit with any of the evidence. The tape recording alone proves she was involved throughout the murder, and not downstairs watching out the window making sure nobody comes to the house as she claimed.

BRADY'S STORY

Brady said that Myra picked up Lesley at the fair by herself and was with her in the car when they picked up Brady, who was a few blocks away from the fair. The three of them went back to Myra and Brady's new home. We don't know the exact chain of events after they arrived. However, we do have a tape recording found by the police chronicling the three of them while they were in one of the bedrooms.

Also, there were pictures of Lesley found later that showed her tied up and wearing a leather outfit, which were thought to have been taken after the tape recording was made. In the nine pictures that were found, Lesley was naked and posed in various ways: such as praying, kneeling and one with her arm stretched out.

Brady also claimed that Myra took part in having sex with Lesley. He said that it was Myra who strangled Lesley with a silk cord while Brady held the girl down. Apparently, Myra would go to the pub afterwards and play with that same silk cord in public.

Brady also claimed that the tub was needed to wash Lesley's body before disposal to remove any hairs or fibers she might have picked up while in their house. The couple then carried the body out to the car, drove out to the moor, and buried Lesley not far from where Pauline Reade's body was.

After they arrived at the Saddleworth Moor, Brady went up over the hill and disappeared in the distance. He had gone to get the spade. Right at that very moment, a policeman pulled up beside Myra, who was waiting by the car, and asked if everything was okay. She was in a panic, as Lesley's body was still in the trunk, but the quick-thinking Myra replied that she was just letting her spark plugs dry out. The officer believed her and drove off.

Myra then drove to where she had left her grandmother earlier that day. It was after 11 p.m. when she finally arrived there. She knocked on the door, and when her uncle answered the door, she told him about how bad the roads were, and that's why she couldn't get there sooner. Myra then told her uncle that it would be way too dangerous to drive her grandma home now, which caused the two of them to argue, as Myra was still going to drive home, so why couldn't she take her grandma with her?

Myra left alone anyways so that she could get back home to Brady and do their regular ritual of burning all the clothes and evidence left at their home. Her grandmother ended up having to sleep on the floor at her son's house. It would be the next morning at around 10:30 when Myra would go pick up her grandmother.

*****

TRANSCRIPT OF THE TAPE RECORDING

BRADY - "Get out of the fucking road! Get in the fucking basket!"

The sound of a door banging, then some heavy footsteps crossing a floor, then somebody blowing into a microphone. A few more footsteps followed with a very quiet woman's voice, so soft that it's not understandable.

In the distance you can hear some more footsteps lightly walking across the room. Some light whispered conversation was happening at the same time.

LESLEY ANN DOWNEY (10-year-old girl) -"Don't! Mum - - ah!" followed by a high-pitched little girl's scream.

HINDLEY - "Shut up!"

LESLEY - "Oh, please. Oh, help."

HINDLEY - "Shh. Shh. Shut up!"

You could now hear the little girl scream loudly again.

HINDLEY - "Shut up. Shut up."

You could hear a gurgling sound and then the child began to cry.

HINDLEY - "Keep quiet and you'll be alright. Go on."

The sound of heavy footsteps running up some stairs and then entering the room while the child continued to cry.

BRADY - "Here."

HINDLEY - "Hush hush, go on."

The child continued to cry lightly, almost like a moaning sound.

HINDLEY - "You are alright, hush, hush. Put it in your mouth, hush and shift that hand."

The child continued crying.

HINDLEY - "Put it in your mouth and keep it in and you'll be alright. Put it in! Stop it. If you don't shh."

The child was now making a muffled sound.

BRADY - "Put it in" at the same time the woman screamed "Put it in."

BRADY - "Put it in, keep it in. Stop it now! Stop it now!"

HINDLEY - "I'm only doing this, and you'll be alright. Put it in your mouth. Put it in, in!"

You could hear Brady and the woman talking with each other quietly, but too low to hear what they are saying.

HINDLEY - "Will you stop it, stop it! Shut!"

BRADY - "Quick, put it in now!"

You could now hear a whimpering from the child, and then a retching sound, almost like someone trying to throw up.

LESLEY - "What's this in for?"

BRADY - "Put it in."

LESLEY - "Can I just tell you something? I must tell you something. Please take your hands off me a minute, please, please, mummy please. I can't tell you."

The child let out a loud grunt.

LESLEY - "I can't tell you, I can't breathe. I can't, Dad will you take your hands off me?"

BRADY - "No, tell me."

LESLEY - "Please God."

BRADY - "Tell me."

LESLEY - "I can't while you got your hands on me."

BRADY - "Why don't you keep it in?"

LESLEY - "Why? What are you going to do with me?"

BRADY - "I want some photographs, that's all. Put it in."

LESLEY - "Don't undress me, will you?"

HINDLEY - "That's right, don't—"

LESLEY - "It hurts me. I want to see mummy, honest to God."

BRADY - "Put it in!"

LESLEY - "I swear on the Bible."

BRADY - "Put it in and hurry up now! The quicker you do this, the quicker you'll get home."

LESLEY - "I've got to go, because I'm going out with my mamma. Leave me, please. Help me will you?"

BRADY - "Put it in your mouth and you'll be alright."

LESLEY - "Will you let me go when this is out?"

BRADY - "Yes. The longer it takes you to do this, the longer it takes you to get home."

LESLEY - "What are you going to do with me first?"

BRADY - "I'm going to take some photographs. Put it in your mouth."

LESLEY - "What for?"

BRADY - "Put it in your mouth, right in."

LESLEY - "I'm not going to do it."

BRADY - "Put it in. If you don't get that hand down, I'll slit your neck!"

LESLEY - "Wont you let me go? Please."

BRADY - "No, no. Put it in, stop talking. What's your name?"

LESLEY - "Lesley."

BRADY - "Lesley what?"

LESLEY - "Ann."

BRADY - "What's your second name?"

LESLEY - "Westford. Westford."

BRADY - "Westford?"

LESLEY - "I have to get home before 8 o'clock. I got to get, or I'll get killed if I don't. Honest to God."

BRADY - "Yes."

The sound of the woman's footsteps walking out of the room and going down some stairs, some clicks and then the woman coming back up the stairs and into the room again.

BRADY - "What is it?"

HINDLEY - "I've left the light on."

BRADY - "You have?"

HINDLEY - "So that -" (the rest of the sentence is not clear enough to tell what she said)

The child then started to cry and said, "It hurts my neck."

BRADY - "Hush, put it in your mouth and you'll be all right."

HINDLEY - "Now listen, stop crying."

LESLEY - "It hurts me."

HINDLEY - "Hush! Shut up, now put it in. Pull that hand away and don't dally and just keep your mouth shut, please. Wait a bit, I'll put this on again. Do you get me?"

LESLEY - "No! I-"

HINDLEY - "Shh, hush. Put that in your mouth, and again packed more solid."

LESLEY - "I want to go home. Honest to God. I'll (muffled speech) before 8 o'clock."

HINDLEY - "No, it's alright."

BRADY - "Eh!"

*****

It was then that music started playing. At first it was some country style music, and then followed by 'Jolly St. Nicholas', then the song 'Little Drummer Boy'. Throughout all the music you could hear muffled noises and people speaking, but their voices were too quiet to hear what they were saying.

Suddenly, there were three loud cracks, even timed and systematic, and the music grew fainter. The last thing you could hear before the tape stopped was some footsteps across the floor.

Meanwhile back at the Downey house, Ann Downey and Alan West were in a panic. Tommy had come home without Lesley. The two of them went to all the neighbors' houses and knocked on doors and searched through the streets looking for her. They returned home at about 10 p.m. with no results, so they called the police.

The next day the police took Alan West, Lesley's soon to be stepfather, in for questioning and he was interrogated for several hours.

CHAPTER 6 - EDWARD EVANS

EDWARD EVANS

On April 24, 1965, David Smith and Maureen Hindley lost their six-month-old baby daughter to bronchitis in the hospital. This led Maureen and David to get more involved with Brady and Myra, as they had no other support from their families, and not really from any other friends.

The two couples started to go to the Saddleworth Moor on a regular basis. The girls would always stay near the car, and the men would head down into the moor. Brady started taking Smith to the places where he had buried the bodies of his previous victims, without letting Smith know. There would be times when Smith would be standing right on top of someone's grave without knowing it.

Brady would also start to give Smith books to read, such as "The Life and Ideas of Marquis de Sade." Brady would emphasize certain passages such as 'should murder be punished by murder?'

Like before, after the four of them left the moor, they would end up back at Myra and Brady's house, where the girls would retire up to bed and the men would stay down in the living room drinking until daylight. This was when Brady started to discuss his plans to commit armed robberies, and asked Smith if he would like to join them.

On one of these nights, October 2, when the men were drinking downstairs, Brady told Smith that he had killed before and had the pictures to prove it. He also claimed that he would do another murder for Smith to prove it.

Tuesday, October 5, Smith returned a box full of books that Brady had lent to him months before, telling him to read them and write down quotes he liked in a separate exercise book. Brady took the books upstairs, and after a few minutes returned with two suitcases. In the suitcases there was the tape recording of Lesley Ann Downing, books of sexual perversions, gun cartridges, and a few letters.

Brady and Myra put the suitcases in the trunk of their car and headed to the Manchester Train Station where they would stow them in a locker. Brady was still unsure about Smith's ability to murder someone. So he thought about taking Smith out for a drive, parking the car, handing him the gun, and telling him to kill a random stranger. If he couldn't do it, then he would shoot Smith. But even Ian knew this idea was not a viable one, as it would lead the police directly to Myra since Smith was married to her sister.

On the morning of October 5, Smith came over and told Brady and Myra that they had received an eviction notice, since they owed 14 pound and 8 shillings. He wanted to borrow the money from them, but Myra told him that they were broke.

Brady then told Smith that they could get the money from "rolling a queer" (i.e. they could go out and find a homosexual, offer him sex if he would come home with them, and steal his money). Because it was still illegal to be homosexual at that time, the person they mugged would be less likely to go the police.

This was going to be the first time that the couple didn't followed their master plan crime list and Brady did not use his Tarot cards to predict what would happen.

Edward Evans was a 17-year-old apprentice engineer, who lived in the Ardwick area of Manchester with his mother Edith, father John, and one sister and brother. On

October 6, 1965, at 6:30 p.m., Edward decided he would go out for the night with his friend, Michael Mahone, to see a soccer game at the Old Trafford soccer stadium. He was wearing a white t-shirt, blue jeans, brown Italian dress shoes, and a suede jacket.

Edward was to meet his friend at a place called 'Auntie's Bar.' According to the owner of the bar, George Smith, Edward showed up around 7 p.m., but his friend Michael never did. Edward ended up leaving the bar to go to the game alone.

Meanwhile, that same evening at about 10:30 p.m., Myra and Ian went out to the store to get some wine. They drove to the Manchester Train Station and parked. Ian went into the station while Myra waited in the car. However, she had parked on a double yellow line. A policeman came by and told her to move, and that if she was still there when he returned, he would ticket her.

When Brady went into the station, he immediately recognized a young man who was standing alone leaning against a wall beside a cigarette machine. Brady had seen him at a Manchester gay pub a couple of times before, but the two had never spoken.

Brady walked over to the man and they chatted for a few minutes. The man was Edward Evans. According to Brady, he asked Edward to come back to his place for a drink, which was really a covert way of inviting him home to have sex.

Edward agreed and the two of them got into the car with Myra. Brady told Edward that Myra was his sister to avoid any suspicion. When they arrived home, Brady told Myra to go get Smith and tell him to come over. When they got out of the car, Brady was able to whisper to Myra to wait a while before they came home.

Up to now the stories from Myra, Brady and Smith were the same, but as with the other murders, they changed when it came to the rape and murder.

MYRA'S STORY

Myra insisted that Smith was waiting at home fully dressed, and that she had no idea about any plan to murder Evans. When she arrived at Smith's place, Maureen was surprised to see her sister and

wanted to know why she was coming over so late. Myra said that she had a message from their mother, who wanted to come around Friday and borrow a pair of Maureen's shoes.

Myra then added that she asked Smith to walk her back to her place since it was dark out and the lights outside the apartment building were not on. The lights being out that night was actually true and confirmed at the trial by the corporation that runs the building.

Smith put on his shoes and told Maureen that he would be back soon. Smith also took the stick that he used when he walked his dog, which was about two inches thick and three feet long with string wrapped around the end of it.

When they arrived at Ian and Myra's home, Myra told Smith to wait across the street until she flashed the kitchen lights twice. Then he was to come in through the front door. Myra disappeared around the back of the house, and Smith waited anxiously.

Brady gave her the signal that the murder was about to happen. Myra went into the kitchen, flashed the lights twice for Smith to enter, and claimed that she never came out again until the murder was over and all the noise had stopped. She claimed her part in the murder was getting the blankets that the men wrapped the body in, and ensuring her grandmother was asleep. She yelled down to the men when it was safe to bring the body upstairs and place it in the spare room.

She said the three of them spent three hours cleaning the living room and made plans of how and where they would dispose of the body the next night. David Smith then left for his home around 3 a.m.

BRADY'S STORY

Brady and Evans went into the house and they opened a bottle of wine, sat down on the sofa and started to talk. Myra went upstairs and changed, and then went over to get Smith. It only took the two men a few minutes before they started to have sex, starting with kissing and then oral sex. Later when trial was held, forensic evidence (dog hairs) from the house was found on Smith's anus and legs after his jeans were removed from his corpse.

Shortly after the men finished, they put their clothes back on and continued to drink. Just then they could hear Myra and Smith coming up the front stairs approaching the front door. Brady bounced up quickly and ran to the front door and opened it.

Brady looked at Smith and said loudly "Do you still want those miniatures? They are in the kitchen." The couple walked in the front door and headed down the hallway and into the kitchen. Brady went back into the living room and walked behind the sofa where Evans was still seated.

Brady then claimed that he had an axe lying under the sofa, and that he reached down, picked it up, and brought it down with great force onto Evans' head. He was aiming for the back of his head to kill him instantly, but Evans turned around at the last second. This caused the axe blade to bounce off Evans' crown.

Evans started screaming out, so Brady kept swinging the axe. Myra and Smith came out of the kitchen and just stood and watched. The dogs that were in the kitchen were barking uncontrollably.

Myra's grandmother, sleeping upstairs, was awakened by all the commotion and shouted down the stairs asking what was happening. Brady said that Myra shouted something back at her grandmother, but he couldn't remember what Myra said, as his mind was focused on killing Evans.

After a dozen blows to his head, Evans was still alive, so Brady went into the kitchen and grabbed some electrical cord. He came back out into the living room, and strangled Evans to death by wrapping the wire around his neck. Evans finally went quiet; Brady stood up and handed the axe to Smith. Brady said later he did this to make sure Smith's prints were on the handle.

The walls, floors, and carpets were spattered with blood. Brady then said, "This is the messiest murder I have committed." He reached down and took Evans' wallet from his jeans and opened it up to look through it. He then took the wallet, Evans' shoes and the axe, and put everything into a large travel bag.

Brady, who had sprained his left ankle sometime during the night, decided that they would put Evans' body upstairs in the spare bedroom. He took the string that was on the end of Smith's dog stick and tied Evans' body into a fetal position. Myra spread a white cotton blanket on the floor. Brady and Smith placed the body in the middle of it and wrapped it up. They wrapped the body again in a plastic sheet, as well as another blanket.

The two men carried the body up to the empty spare bedroom while Myra held onto the door handle of her grandmother's door, just in case she decided to get up. Brady claimed that he had to take his holster and gun off and put them down in the bedroom, as they got in his way when they were moving the body. He said that had he remembered to retrieve the gun, he could have used it on the police when they later came to search the house.

The three of them spent almost three hours cleaning up all the blood in the living room. Brady would comment later that he thought it was incompetence that the police couldn't find traces of blood in the carpet.

Smith then left for his home, and Brady was very happy with how calm Smith handled himself during the murder. Brady and Myra drank wine until about 3:30 a.m. that night before falling asleep. It was then that Brady thought there would be no rush to bury the body, as there was nothing to connect them to the victim. He then thought he might like to burn Evans' remains on their next bonfire night.

DAVE SMITH'S STORY

"Brady opened the door and he said in a very loud voice "Do you want those miniatures?" I nodded my head to say yes and he led me into the kitchen and gave me three

miniature bottles of spirits and said, "Do you want the rest?"

When I first walked into the house, the door to the living room was closed. Ian went into the living room and I waited in the kitchen. I waited about a minute or two then suddenly I heard a hell of a scream, it sounded like a woman, high-pitched. Then the screams carried on, one after another, loud. Then I heard Myra shout, "Dave, help him!" very loud.

When I ran in, I just stood inside the living room and I saw a young lad. He was lying with his head and shoulders on the couch and his legs were on the floor. He was facing upwards. Ian was standing over him, facing him, with his legs on either side of the young lad's legs.

The lad was still screaming. Ian had a hatchet in his hands. He was holding it above his head, and he hit the lad on the left side of his head with the hatchet. I heard the blow, it was a terribly hard blow, it sounded horrible."

According to Smith, Brady persuaded him to help dispose of the body since he sprained his ankle in the fight with Evans and couldn't do it himself. Smith wasn't strong enough to carry Evans to Brady's car, so they decided to put the body upstairs in the spare bedroom with Smith assuring Brady that he would indeed help him dispose of the corpse later.

Smith claims he was scared that Brady would kill him once they were finished, but Brady told him he could go. On Smith's way home, he was so nervous about Brady attacking him, he would jump and yelp at any noise he heard.

Maureen was sleeping in their bedroom when Smith walked in. He went straight to the bathroom, started wildly throwing up, and moaned loudly, almost like a painful cry. This woke up Maureen, who joined him in the bathroom. As she started to rub his back, she noticed that he was covered in blood.

"What happened!" she screamed in panic. Smith slowly stammered out that he had witnessed a murder, and that it was her sister Myra and Brady that did the murder. Maureen fell into a deep shock but told him that they had to go to the police.

Smith agreed but was still terrified of the rage he saw in Brady's eyes when he killed Evans. He was worried that Brady would be watching them from their house, and if he saw them leaving, he would come after them. The couple decided that they would wait until daylight, when there would be lots of people out on the road, and they would have a better chance to get away.

At 6 a.m., they slipped out the front door. Smith was armed with a kitchen knife, and Maureen had a screwdriver. When they got to the nearest telephone booth, Smith called the police and explained to them what he had witnessed the previous night.

A squad car drove to the booth and picked the couple up and took them to the police station for questioning. After Smith explained to the officer what he had witnessed, they called superintendent Bob Talbot, who was a well-known criminal detective in Britain.

Talbot met with Sergeant Carr and headed to the house where the murder was alleged to have happened. Smith told them that Brady had at least two guns and would leave the house to go to work at 8:30 a.m. Talbot decided he would arrange for 24 uniformed officers to attend the house while they searched.

Talbot and the other officers made it to the location and waited to catch Brady as he was leaving for work. After 8:30 came and went and no Brady, he decided he would approach the house. He saw a deliveryman dropping off loaves of bread down the street, so he borrowed his white delivery jacket before knocking on Brady's door.

Talbot went around to the back of the house and knocked on the back door. Myra answered the door and seemed surprised to see a bread man at the door.

DETECTIVE: "Is your husband in?"

MYRA: "I haven't got a husband."

DETECTIVE: "I am a police superintendent and I have reason to believe there is a man in the house."

MYRA: "There's no man here."

DETECTIVE: "I have received a report that an act of violence took place here last night and we are investigating it."

MYRA:" There's nothing wrong here."

Talbot pushed passed Myra while taking off his white coat, and she then realized that he was indeed a detective.

MYRA: "He's in the other room. He's in the other room in bed."

The detective entered the living room and found Brady seated on a sofa that was pushed up against the wall, with no back on it. He was wearing a string-vest and had a surprised look on his face. Myra claimed later that the moment the detective walked into the living room, and she saw Brady staring in shock, she finally felt free.

Talbot looked around the room and had a sergeant look through the kitchen. Brady had an exercise book in front of him and a ballpoint pen. After Talbot introduced himself and told him the reason they were there, Ian started writing.

Talbot turned to Myra and said he wanted to search upstairs, so Myra led him to the staircase. The two walked up to the top landing, and Talbot tried the first door. It opened, and inside, sitting and drinking some tea, was Myra's grandmother. He excused himself, closed her door and walked to the next room. When he tried the door, it was locked. He asked Myra if she had the key.

Myra explained that the room was always locked as she kept her firearms in there, and she had left her key at work. The two walked down the stairs and into the hallway. Talbot told her that he wasn't going to leave until he was able to check the locked. room. He offered to send an officer to her workplace to get the key. Myra said nothing.

BRADY: "You better give him the key. A fight got out of hand last night. It's upstairs." This was his hint to Myra so that she would know what story to go with when they found the body. The two walked back up the stairs, and this time Myra unlocked the door and swung it open.

The room was set up like a regular spare bedroom with a bed, dresser and an armchair. The detective noticed under the window that there was a large parcel covered up with a blanket. He walked closer to it and saw a travel bag sitting beside the end of the blanket. It was open and had a bloody axe in it.

Talbot went back down the stairs and told Brady to get dressed. He asked two officers to watch over him.

Brady and Myra had a plan just in case they got caught. They would shoot the police in the head first, then Brady would kill Myra, then put the gun in his own mouth and kill himself. The two detectives could have been killed if they had been able to carry out their plan. Fortunately, because Brady had left his gun upstairs while he and Smith moved the body, Brady wasn't armed.

The neighbors were all out on their front lawns looking on as more police started showing up to the Brady house. Brady was escorted out to the police car wearing handcuffs. Myra's grandmother was confused as to what was happening, and Myra walked her over to their neighbors.

CHAPTER 7 – THE INVESTIGATION

IAN BRADY TAKEN INTO CUSTODY BY POLICE

Myra Hindley was not arrested with Ian Brady, but she demanded to go with him to the police station. She took her dog, Puppet, to the station with her. Hindley refused to make a statement beyond her claim that Evans' death had been an accident.

A female detective, Margaret Campion, in the police station restaurant, questioned Myra. Myra wanted food for her dog, but the detective told her that she would only give the dog food if she would answer some questions.

Myra kept repeating the same lines over and over. *"I didn't do it, Ian didn't do it. I am saying nothing. Ask Ian. Whatever Ian has done, I have done."*

Myra gave saliva and blood samples to the police. She also asked her mother to bring her some clothing, as the police were going to retain the clothes she was wearing to test forensically. Myra wasn't charged at the time and left with her mother, with whom she would stay.

Back at Myra and Brady's house, the police had roped off the property and refused entry to anyone. They searched the house inside and out, and even dug three feet deep in the garden. Not much of note was retrieved from the house except for Brady's notebook, where detective Talbot noticed that Brady had written the name of John Kilbride in it.

It would be another four days, on October 11, 1965, before the police would arrest Myra as well. She was taken to the Risley Detention Center and charged as an accessory to Evans' murder. During those four days, Hindley burned papers and envelopes that belonged to Brady in an ashtray. She later claimed that they contained the plans for the robberies they were going to do, as well as the master plans for their murders. She also asked that Millward's fire both her and Brady so they could receive unemployment benefits. There was only one piece of evidence that she was unable to retrieve - the train station ticket for the two suitcases that was left in the house now under police restriction due to the ongoing investigation.

Brady finally confessed to the murder of Edward Evans, but said that it was him and Smith that did it, and Hindley had nothing to do with it. Brady made an official statement:

'Last night I met Eddie in Manchester. We were drinking and then we went home to Hattersley. We had an argument and we came to blows. After the first few blows the situation got out of control. When the argument started, Dave Smith was at the front door and Myra called him in. Eddie kicked me at the beginning on the ankle. There was a hatchet on the floor, and I hit Eddie with it. After that the only noise Eddie made was a gurgling. When Dave and I began cleaning up the floor the gurgling stopped. The we tied up the body, Dave and I, nobody else helped. Dave and I carried it upstairs. Then we sat in the house until three or four in the morning. Then we decided to get rid of the body in the morning, early the next day or next night.'

The day after his arrest, on Thursday, October 7, Brady was formerly charged with the murder of Edward Evans and made a short appearance in court the next day.

On Monday, October 11, at 3 p.m., the police arrested Myra for the murder of Edward Evans, as forensics had determined that Evans' blood was on both Brady and Myra's clothes. One of Myra's shoes also had blood drops from Evans, which would mean that she was in the room when he was being murdered. If the blood had been smears instead of droplets, it could have been from her helping to clean up the mess.

While the police were questioning Smith, he told them about helping Brady gather anything that might be incriminating at their house and placing it all into suitcases. He also told them that Brady had met Evans at a train station, and that was a place he would look for murder victims. This led police to check out all the local train stations. On October 15, the police discovered a locker rented by Brady at the Manchester Central station, and inside of the locker they found Brady's suitcase. Inside the suitcase, the police found nine photographs of a naked, tied up girl, and a tape recording of her screaming and pleading to go home to her mom's. This was later to be identified as that of 10-year-old Lesley Ann Downey.

They also found several pictures of the Saddleworth Moor and a notepad of Brady's that had the name of a missing 10-year-old boy, John Kilbride. An 11-year-old neighbor of Brady's, Pat Hodges, had told the police that he had been taken to the moor by the couple once. It wasn't long before the police connected the moor to the missing boy and began to do a search of the land with 150 officers.

Brady told Detective Talbot that Smith had hesitated telling the police about the suitcases because there was incriminating evidence of Smith being involved in the murder. Smith was really upset and stressed over this statement, until the police came to an agreement with him that he would be immune from prosecution for helping them convict Brady and Myra.

When the detectives confronted Brady with the tapes of Lesley Ann Downey being attacked, he told them that he had taken the photos of Downey, but that she had left their house alive with David Smith and another man that had been waiting outside in a car. Myra was then presented with the same tapes, where she reacted by crying when they played the tape. She then refused to say anything, as she knew Brady was going to tell a story.

Door-to-door canvassing by the police led to the discovery that the couple often went to the Saddleworth Moor. A neighbour witnessed them going there many times. The police ordered a search of the moor with over 150 officers and volunteers.

On October 16, around 3 p.m., one of the officers, Robert Spiers, was searching the moor and went over to a private area to relieve himself. He noticed what looked like a bone sticking out of the ground. He called over to Detective Talbot, and the two men started digging with their bare hands until they found what looked like a person's arm. It appeared as if some animals had dug up the remains and ravaged what they could from the body.

It was Lesley Ann Downey's body they had found first, identified by her mother Ann the following day. Her mother was shown only a few body parts that were not torn and chewed on by animals. Ann had to listen to the tape of her daughter's attack by Brady and Myra. She was also shown pictures of Brady, whom she couldn't identify. Alan West, the girl's stepfather, was not a blood relative and not allowed to identify the body. He was thought of as a suspect the whole time, and was unable to live a normal life, as their neighbors and friends would avoid talking to him.

On Thursday, October 21, both Brady and Hindley were charged with the murder of Lesley Ann Downey. Detective Talbot noticed that in one of the pictures they found in the suitcases, Myra and her dog were posing only a few feet from where they found the body of Lesley. He started to wonder if they had taken pictures at every place that they buried a body.

The police then took Hindley's dog, Puppet, to be examined by a veterinarian, so they could determine the age of the dog. They would then use that to compare to the pictures at the moor that Brady had, to see if they could put them in a sequence of when they were each taken. Unfortunately, the dog died when they administered an anaesthetic. This made Hindley furious. Hindley sent a letter to her mother from prison saying that her heart had been torn to pieces and that she believed the police had murdered her pet.

The detectives then went to the moor and searched for each of the locations in the pictures where Myra had posed. When they found a location that matched one of the pictures, they started poking into the ground with sticks. They would pull the stick out of the ground and smell for the scent of a dead body. Within two pokes, Detective Chaddock smelled putrefaction that made him want to vomit. They had located the remains of John Kilbride.

Also on October 21, the grave of John Kilbride was found at the exact spot Hindley had posed for one of Brady's pictures at the moor. The police had John's mother, Sheila Kilbride, identify the body and clothing of her son. On December 2, 1965, Brady was charged with a third murder, that of John Kilbride, while Myra was only charged as an accessory to the murder.

Brady and Hindley were held at Risley, which was about thirty miles from their home.

In November 1965, the abolition of the Death Penalty Act was passed, therefore leaving the crown only able to seek life imprisonment for Brady and Hindley.

Brady and Hindley decided that they would get married, as married prisoners were allowed contact with each other, but the application was turned down. The couple would send each other letters that were written in German. In one of these letters, Brady asked Myra to send him a stimulating letter, as in sexually arousing, about subjects such as causing pain to children.

CHAPTER 8 – TRIAL

MOB OF PEOPLE GATHERED AROUND THE COURTHOUSE WHEN BRADY AND HINDLEY ARRIVED

The trial began on April 19, 1966, and lasted for two weeks. The courtroom was presided over by Judge Fenton Atkinson. The courtroom had to be fitted with safety glass to protect both Hindley and Brady, as there had been so many threats issued by the public. It was also to protect the prosecutors and witnesses who were against Brady, as he would attempt to spit on them as they walked by on their way to the stand to testify.

Just as Brady and Hindley were brought to the courthouse, two figures covered with blankets jumped on the police car that carried them. The two were arrested and it ended up being Patrick and Terry Downey, the father and uncle of victim Lesley Ann Downey. The two men were eventually released but told that if they returned to the court, they would be charged.

Both Hindley and Brady had been charged with three murders - Downey, Kilbride, and Evans. Each of the defendants had their own defense lawyer. Brady's lawyer was David Lloyd Adamson and Myra's lawyer was Phillip Curtis. Brady appeared in court wearing a grey suit, white shirt and a vest. Myra appeared in a black and white spotted suit with a yellow blouse, and she still wore her hair bleached blonde.

The couple had pleaded not guilty to all charges, which was no surprise. The whole trial would last 15 days and was heard in an open court so that anybody could watch. There were over 150 pieces of evidence and 86 witnesses called to testify.

The prosecutor, William Mars-Jones was using Dave Smith as the chief witness, and he testified for about seven hours. Smith was now 18 years old and showed up in tight jeans and a velvet shirt. The prosecution made him go and put on a tie during a break in the proceedings. It would be revealed after the trial that Smith was to be paid an enormous sum for his exclusive story, but only if the couple were convicted. Judge Atkinson called this a gross interference with the course of justice.

Maureen Hindley appeared in a new suit and a bouffant hairstyle. She testified that her sister Myra had changed after meeting and going out with Brady. It was as though she was trying to tell the court that Myra was a sweet and innocent woman who had been warped by Brady. Under cross-examination she was asked about receiving 100 pounds for giving a story to the newspapers. She admitted to it, but said it never changed her story.

David and Maureen Smith's admission for being paid by a newspaper for their stories was not damaging for the prosecution and seemed to have no effect on the jury.

Brady testified for eight hours, and Hindley for six hours. Hindley claimed throughout the trial that she was not responsible for any of the murders. She also claimed that she was not present in the room on the tape of Downey being tortured. She claimed that she was looking out the window and running a bath the whole time that Brady was with Downey.

The prosecutor spent a lot of time emphasising Brady's fascination with Nazi paraphernalia – the books and tapes that he owned. Brady responded that his fascination with Hitler and the Nazis was aesthetically based, not political. He had admired the boldness and courage with which Hitler put his beliefs into effect in Germany.

Brady admitted to killing Evans with an axe, but insisted that Evans died from strangulation, not the axe blows, and therefore he wasn't the one who killed him. The jury then heard the tapes of Lesley Ann Downey being assaulted and having her pictures taken by Brady and Myra. The prosecutor explained that in the tape when Myra and Brady were shouting at Lesley to 'put it in', they were talking about Brady's penis, not a gag.

The jury retired to deliberate at 2:40 p.m. on May 6 and asked for three pieces of evidence. Brady's notebook, the disposal plan for Evans' body, and Myra's shoes that had Evans' spotted blood on them. Two hours later, the jury asked for the dates that Myra bought her guns. The jury returned with their verdict by 5 p.m. that night.

On May 6, the jury found Brady guilty of all three murders and Hindley guilty of only two of the murders (Downey and Evans).

The judge asked the couple to stand and wanted to know if they had anything to say before sentencing. Brady said, "No, except that the guns were bought in July 1964." He then buttoned up his suit jacket and turned to look at Myra, who said nothing.

The judge then handed down sentencing:

"Ian Brady, these were three calculated, cruel, cold-blooded murders. In your case I pass the only sentence which the law now allows, which is three concurrent sentences of life imprisonment. Put him down."

"In your case, Hindley, you have been found guilty of two equally horrible murders, and in the third as an accessory after the fact. On the two murders, the sentence is two concurrent sentences of life imprisonment, and on the charge of being an accessory after the fact to the death of Kilbride, a concurrent sentence of seven years imprisonment. Put her down."

Two days after they were sentenced, the judge released a letter to the Home Secretary:

"Though I believe Brady is wicked beyond belief without hope of redemption, I cannot feel that the same is necessarily true of Hindley once she is removed from his influence. At present, she is as deeply corrupted as Brady, but it is not so long

ago that she was taking instruction in the Roman Catholic Church and was a communicant and a normal sort of girl."

After the sentencing, Brady and Hindley spent one more night at Risley before being sent off to prison. They could speak to each other one last time, only briefly in the hallway, before being taken away. Myra claimed that she only asked Brady not to kill himself in prison.

Myra Hindley was sent to Holloway Prison in London and Ian Brady went to Durham prison. They would never see each other again.

CHAPTER 9 – PRISON

POLICE SEARCHING THE MOOR FOR THE BODIES OF BRADY AND HINDLEY'S VICTIMS

Brady wrote his first letter to Myra on his sixth day in Durham Prison:

"Dear Myra, it's a beautiful morning, clear blue sky, a sharp early tang in the air and

the sun's radiance hot on the skin. There's an old clock tower near here, the chimes ring out every quarter of an hour, that sound combined with the warbling of the birds helps to produce a pleasant backdrop and reduce the stark realities of the present cheerful country sounds."

I work in my cell during the day sewing mailbags, which may not be an ideal mode of work but it's surprising how quickly time goes while doing it. Well, Myra, I hope you've gotten over the initial shock of your sentence. I at least got what I expected but you should never have been on any charge except for harboring. Keep your chin up. The day you are released will be the happiest day of my life. I expect none happier."

"So, clear your mind of well-justified hate and bitterness and approach each day in hope and each person as an individual. Never express despair, you have a future and I will see you begin life anew, and so, I'll dwell once more in freedom as seen through your eyes. But for now, keep your eyes looking towards the sky, ignore the grimy ground till you again tread grass underfoot. I'm counting on you, by gaining your freedom, to bring me back to life. So, don't let me down, Kiddo."

Brady signed off *"Ich werde sie nicht vergessen"* (German for 'I will not forget you').

Myra responded about one week later, but she was not so positive about her experiences in jail:

"I don't for a minute think they'll grant my appeal, but I have nothing to lose by trying, and what's a year, with sentences like ours? Anyway, I've been convicted and branded a murderess, so I'm not just sitting back and accepting it. We know each other, and one day, in the fullness of time, the truth will out. It must be so. I dreamed last night that Smith had died, or left Maureen, and she came forward and said that she lied about Ashton Market etc. She had her baby last week, a boy. I think her conscience will start bothering her pretty soon."

"Here I am, Sunday, 7:30 p.m. there's a strong wind blowing, rattling the leaves on the many trees in the gardens outside my cell. It sounds just like home. There's a weeping willow in the center of the lane. I feel rather like one myself tonight. I feel desolate, not because I'm on my own of course, but because you aren't here. I miss you all the time, but sometimes more than others. I hate Sundays anyway."

"You've read, of course, about all the publicity concerning the girl at school whose mother kept her off because she wasn't allowed to wipe her cutlery on a napkin? I read yesterday that the people have bought her story for 800 pounds and the BBC have paid her 130 pounds. What a waste of money."

I'll sign off again until tomorrow. I wear wax earplugs some nights. The girl in the next room sometimes spends her nights crying for *her sister, so I put plugs in and cut that noise off. This cell is perfect for peace and quiet. I wish I could remain here indefinitely, however if I move to the star wing, I hope to remain under rule 43,* (isolation from fellow prisoners as they were both child sex offenders) *and cherish any solitude, it suits me fine."*

Myra Hindley appealed her convictions in 1966 but was denied. She wrote letters to Brady once a week. He wrote Myra every Friday until March 1972, when she wrote to Brady telling him that their love affair was over. She had started to believe in God, and he would never accept such a change in her.

Myra then applied to be placed into general population, which was granted, so she could now walk around in prison without any escorts. The first thing that she did with her newfound freedom was to enrol in the Open University to take a Humanities degree class.

In January 1973, Myra had found a new love, a lesbian prison officer, Patricia Cairns. The two of them became quite close very fast, and by November devised a plan to help Myra escape from prison. They had the dream of going to Brazil to work as missionaries.

Maxine Croft, a 22-year-old inmate, was in the same prison as Myra for three years for writing bad checks. Croft was also a prison trustee who was brought into the escape plan by Cairns. As a prison trustee, Croft had access to parts of the prison that were out of bounds for most prisoners. She was allowed day paroles to London. Croft returned from her outing realizing that she was almost free, and was so stressed that she ended up telling prison officials about Cairn's plan to get Myra out of prison.

Patricia Cairns was fired from her job at the prison, arrested, and charged with conspiring to affect the escape of Myra Hindley. All three of them went to trial in April 1974, and all pleaded guilty to the charges. Cairns was given a six-year sentence, Maxine Croft got an extra 18 months, and Myra got an additional 12 months added to her sentence. Maxine appealed her sentenced and won, and was released immediately.

In 1983, David Astor, who was a friend of Myra's defense attorney, Frank Longford, started to make visits to see Myra. Astor was also giving her money, hidden by the church.

Ian Brady was sent to prison, where he spent nearly two decades, until he was moved to the Ashworth Psychiatric Hospital, which is a high security facility. He was diagnosed as a psychopath. He repeatedly stated that he did not ever want to be released, and that he wanted to be allowed to die. Brady went on a hunger strike in 1999, and had to be force fed, and this continued right through until 2012.

Brady claimed that the murders were not part of a never-ending series of serial killings, but merely an existential exercise.

Brady also claimed that he and Hindley had moved past the murders by the end of 1964 and had wanted to commit armed robberies in the future.

Brady published a book through Feral Publishing in the United States in 2001. It was titled "The Gates of Janus". It contains his analyses of several serial killers.

Madame Tussaud's in London sent a letter to Brady asking for his personal details such as eye color, etc. and a set of his clothes as they were making a wax model of him for their 'House of Horrors.'

On November 29, 1984, a 'Sunday People' journalist, Fred Harrison, was the first person in nine years to be allowed to visit Brady. Harrison made a report that he thought that Brady looked at least 90 years old. It was on his second visit to Brady that he was told about the murders of Pauline Reade and Keith Bennett, and that they had been committed by Brady and Myra.

It would take several more visits to get more of the details about these murders and other murders that Brady was involved in, that nobody else knew anything about. Harrison started to publish his findings in a series of articles called 'My Secret Murders' in June of 1985. When Brady heard about the articles, he would no longer accept visits from Harrison. Harrison went on to publish a book about one year later called 'Brady and Hindley: Genesis of the Moor Murders.'

What Brady had confessed to about the murders of Reade and Bennett was not about clearing his conscience, or trying to give some relief to the victim's families. It was more of a selfish nature. In 1985, Myra had applied for parole and rumors were that she might get approved for it. So Brady decided he would act. Brady confessed the two of them killed at least two others. This made the parole board deny Myra's application.

The relatives of Pauline Reade and Keith Bennett had read the articles written by Harrison, and were impatient for the police to reopen the cases and find their loved one's remains. They insisted that the police bring Brady and Myra back to the moor to show them where they buried the bodies.

In the winter of 1986, Myra Hindley received a letter from Bennett's mother, Winnie, in which she asked Hindley for help locating her son's remains. Some say she was so moved by this letter, she decided to help. Others say Myra heard about Brady's confession, and wanted to get sole credit for discovering the bodies, which might lead to her getting out on probation.

Hindley then made a 17-hour tape confessing to the police, in which she described all five murders in great detail. She was taken to the moor twice so that she could show the police where the bodies were buried, but for three months nothing was found.

Myra was taken to the moor to look for the remains the first time on December 16, 1986, first to the airport in the early morning and then to the moor by police helicopter. There was a leak to the press when this was to happen, so there were reporters all over the moor and even a helicopter rented by the press.

Myra was taken a second time to the moor on March 24, 1987, where she spent most of the time being walked around the areas that she had pointed out on the first visit. Myra's taped confession would be released to the public in the next month, so police felt pressure to have the bodies of the victims before the public knew.

On July 1, 1987, Pauline Reade's body was found in an area that Hindley had shown the police. It was only about 300 feet from where Lesley Ann Downey's body was found.

After police found Pauline's body, Brady decided he would help the police as well. He was taken to the moor the first time; however, he was not able to find Keith Bennett's grave. Whether he just didn't remember or was taking the police on a wild goose chase was unknown. The search for Bennett was called off on August 24, 1987.

In November 1987, the police got permission to take Brady out to the moor again to see if he would show them where Bennett was buried. On December 8, 1987 at 5 a.m., police took Brady to the moor for a second time. They spent nine hours searching and found nothing.

EPILOGUE

EDWARD EVANS (LAST VICTIM), MYRA HINDLEY WITH RIFLE, IAN BRADY WITH RIFLE AND THEIR DOG, DAVID SMITH AND MAUREEN HINDLEY

Myra Hindley died in prison when she was 60 years old in November 2002 of bronchial pneumonia brought on by heart disease.

Ian Brady died May 15, 2017 in Ashworth Hospital.

Dave Smith was never charged in the murders, but was rumored by the people in Manchester to have played a part in them. Smith was called names and ridiculed by all his neighbors and even strangers that just passed him on the street. One of his neighbors, William Lees, bothered him so much that Smith ended up stabbing him several times and was arrested and sentenced to three years in prison in July 1969. He died in Ireland in 2012.

Maureen Smith decided she would leave Dave when he went to prison. By then, they had three children and she was unable to handle raising them, so she gave them away to government childcare. When Smith got out of prison in 1972, he gained custody of the three children and divorced Maureen in 1973. He then went on to get remarried.

Right after getting custody of his children, Smith was arrested yet again. Dave had been living with his father, who found out that he had cancer, so Dave gave him a milk drink containing over twenty crushed sodium amytal pills, killing his father. Smith ended up spending two days in prison for a mercy killing.

Maureen also remarried, to a man named William Scott, in 1974, who was 22 years older than her, and they had a daughter, Sharon. In 1980, Maureen suffered a brain hemorrhage. Myra was granted permission to visit her in the hospital, but by the time she arrived, Maureen had already passed.

The house on Wardle Brook Avenue that the couple shared was demolished by the local city council in 1987.

Keith Bennett's grave has still not been located.

LETTER ONE - JULY 2015

LETTER ONE HIGHLIGHTS

July 2, 2015

Dear Cody,

Thanks for your letter. Yes, more psychiatrists, criminologist, and merely political parents reinforcing the state line integrally in order to obtain official posts, peers commissioners as reliable rubber stampers. I receive letters from many university students and lecturers asserting that my book 'Gates of Janus' would have been worth ten times more if it was written by FBI profilers, psychiatrists, psychologists etc. all trying to create a media career for themselves by claiming to have a unique insight into the criminal mind. In reality, thinking that they themselves think and act as criminals, not surprising of course as criminal instincts are indications or partially active in the minds of every same person as for always publicly stated, you can't treat honest respectable people when it comes to serial global slaughter and theft as all history illustrates. If you want the real news on Al-Jazeera, a freebie channel on 133 with dozens of political, tribal, social wars etc. raging daily throughout the world. You're about to conclude that most of the same people are in prison. The real underworld of major crime is obviously above politicians, bankers, military, corporate etc. who are all psychopathic or psychotic.

The whole African Continent consists of 50 odd countries run by insane dictators and you need only look as much as Tony Blair and George Bush as recent representations of war criminals in the west. Study the leaders of the world, not the petty criminals in its prisons. The police and the intelligence and military forces that protect the elite status of the establishment, all this is self-evident to many of course, but not the sleepwalkers.

Yes, I know the areas well (Mosley and Greenfield areas in Manchester) leading the hottest field and other major cities north Bolton? Some excellent architecture up in York, up your way. River Abbey is worth a visit. Yes, its academic stereotypical smears that all serial killers mistreat animals, we usually mistreat anyone who did. As documented. Yes, I had a criminal record in Glasgow, and was on an apprenticeship at the shipyard in Golvin, also worked at Smithfield Market in Manchester, but it was someone else who implicated me in a petty crime falsely leading to

Borstal, where I ran gambling and booze. Eventually I worked in the offices as I always insisted that one should have a legal source of income as well.

I was educated at Shaolin's Academy in Glasgow, but again I chose my own path studying psychology and other subjects suitable to my plans.

(Do you make any money from your book?)

No, I'm donating all money for 'Gates of Janus' to charities.

(Can I visit you in prison?)

No, I halted all social visits and phone calls in 1998 when Ashworth (Mental Hospital) became a regressive prison.

(Asked about Manchester)

Yes, Tip Street was always a criminal haunt, running down to Smithfield. The Kings pub on Oldham Street, (Cody used to work the door there).

(asked if he ever visited Germany)

Yes, I visited Berlin, Munich, Hamburg, and Nuremburg.

(Do you have any firearms?)

When police surrounded the house and blocked all roads, I was caught in bed downstairs, while two pistols, a .45 and a .38, and a rifle were all upstairs. Elsewhere we also had a 303 rifle and a Browning 9-millimeter automatic with unlimited ammunition.

(Do you know other areas of Manchester?)

Yes, I know Oldham and Shaw etc. and I enclosed a sign label for sticking in Janus (his book).

Thanks for the envelope Smithfield (Smithfield Market was where Brady worked at one time, and the envelope was a souvenir that Cody sent to him in prison)

(Are you religious?)

No, I'm not religious, as I've said, when men make plans the Gods laugh.

Best Wishes

Ian Stewart Brady

Mr Leary Lachery   Ian Stewart-Brady,

2nd July 15

Dear Leary,

Thanks for your letters and the photos.

Yes, most psychiatrists and criminologists are merely political parrots, reinforcing the state line ingratiatingly, in order to obtain official posts, fees, commissions or reliable rubber stamps. I received letters from many university students and lecturers, asserting that my book, "The Gates of Janus" was "worth ten written by famous FBI profilers, penal psychiatrists/psychologists, etc," all trying to create a lucrative media career for themselves, by claiming to have unique insight into "the criminal mind"! — in reality meaning that they themselves think and act as criminals do. (Not surprising, of course, as criminal instincts are ubiquitous, latent or partially active in the minds of every "sane" citizen. As I've always publicly stated, you can't beat "decent, honest, respectable" people when it comes to serial global slaughter and theft, as all history illustrates! If you watch the real news on Aljazeera (Freeview channel 133), with dozens of political, tribal, racial wars, etc, raging daily throughout the world, you'd perhaps conclude that most of the "sane" people are in prison! The real "underworld" of major crime is obviously above — politicians, bankers, military, corporate, etc, all floridly psychopathic or psychotic. The whole African continent consists of fifty-odd countries run by insane dictators. And you need only look at such as Tony Blair and George Bush as recent representatives of mad criminals in the west! Study the leaders of the world, not the comparatively petty criminals in prisons, and the police and intelligence and military forces which protect and perpetuate the elite status quo of the establishment.

LETTER TWO - AUGUST 2015

LETTER TWO HIGHLIGHTS

August 2, 2015

Dear Cody,

Thank you for your July letters.

No, I didn't authorize any extended edition of the book. I donated the entire proceeds of the first edition to charity, and all future proceeds. So, the publisher by sending me no funds, all royalties for the second edition, and foreign translated editions, is in effect stealing from and defrauding charities of proceeds due to them (the royalties from the first edition of Brady's book all went to charities, the second edition was released by the publisher, Feral House, without Brady signing off on the book, and no royalties were sent to the charities - the publisher claims that it was an extended version).

As for the afterword written by Sotos (*Peter Sotos is a controversial author also published by Feral House*), it was widely attacked by all in the first edition. The publisher paid Sotos to write a deliberate attack in order to placate any right-wing criticisms. Sotos is a convicted pedophile, child pornographer and police informer, and was publicly described as a toilet door scribbler who would produce any picture or obscenity for money, which reflects even more clearly the money grabbing greed and treachery of the publisher of course. (*ironic that Brady is calling out Sotos for being a pedophile, which is what Brady was.*)

Obviously, the death of Colleen Watson (Brady's longtime friend who wrote a forward in Brady's book) in 2014, obviously encouraged Parfrey (*referring to Adam Parfrey, the founder and owner of Feral House*) to increase his fraudulent exploitation to feel free to take any measures of public exposure you think fit in. My solicitors have also been instructed likewise and for legal action. As you know my mighty is right, and prisoners are always exploited both for money and to distract attention from the major criminals in government, corporations, and the military force of law and order.

My solicitors made it plain through the media that Powell (a woman from South Wales who at one time got friendly with Brady, and was telling stories on him) was then entirely dismissed from my legal affairs etc.

(Can I visit you?)

No, as I stated I stopped all visits and phone calls in 1998 when this place became a regressive prison, and despite many of my previous solicitors asking me to reconsider I remain unchanged and without regret in this respect.

Thanks for the envelopes, if you see any Schaefer pen refills in blue medium, I'm running out, just two will do. Please excuse the bedridden hand writing.

Best Wishes

Ian Stewart Brady

Bn'd Cody Lackey   Ian Stewart-Brady

2nd August 15.

Thanks for your July letters.
No, I didn't authorise any extended edition of the book. I donated the entire proceeds of the first edition to charity, and all future proceeds. So the publisher, by sending me no funds of royalties for the second edition and foreign translated editions, is in effect stealing from and defrauding charities of proceeds due to them. As for the "Afterword" by Sotos. It was widely attacked by all in the first edition. The publisher, Parfrey, admitted in writing that, the book having two excellent [+] Introductions by the famous authors Colin Wilson and Dr Alan Keightley, both of whom know and corresponded with me for decades, he paid Sotos to write a deliberate attack, in order to placate any frightening controversy. Sotos, a convicted US paedophile, child pornographer and police informer, was privately described as "a toilet door scribbler who would produce any lie or obscenity for money." Which reflects even more clearly the money-grubbing greed and treachery of the publisher, of course. Obviously the death of Colin Wilson last year encouraged Parfrey to increase his fraudulent exploitation. So feel free to take any measures of exposure you think fit. My solicitors have also been instructed likewise, and for legal actions.
As you know, might is right, and the victor always writes history and dictates morality. So prisoners are naturally exploited, both for money and to distract attention from the major

* Parfrey

113

LETTER THREE - OCTOBER 2015

LETTER THREE HIGHLIGHTS

October 12, 2015

Dear Cody,

Thanks for your letter.

(Cody had sent Brady a Christmas card and a bracelet with the flag of Scotland on it.)

The Christmas card you sent was held by Mercy Care POA. And the bracelet was also not permitted. I instructed the thief executive (it should be 'Chief' executive, but Brady was upset) office to return both prohibited items to you, so let me know when you receive them. You shouldn't bother sending in any other items as all the attention-seeking officials without real jobs here will simply prohibit items to justify their own parasitic existences.

Second, it is common knowledge that the more corrupt, the more covertly corrupt and criminal the person is in our system, the more publicly moral and righteous they appear to the ignorant. Yes, I'm still bedridden and now I have a chest infection as I've said my solicitors and London legal executives will handle my funeral arrangements and I've been kept informed.

(Cody had offered to do security at Brady's funeral with members of the criminal underworld - it wasn't a genuine offer, it was to find out Brady's plans for his funeral and to see if Brady trusted Cody enough to get access to his body and his estate)

I'm glad you took my advice and avoided approaches by the media (in the previous letter you will read about Cody's offer to be on the Jeremy Kyle Show - Cody told Brady that he turned down the offer due to Brady's advice not to go on the show). In my day, people actually went out of their way rather than speak to the media. Quite the opposite these days. As you said, the Andy Warhol prediction that everybody would be famous for 15 minutes has been surpassed, more like 15 seconds.

(Do you believe prisoners can become institutionalized?)

People that become institutionalized due so because consciously and subconsciously they prefer to be. More at home at prison than in the free, the outside world talking of freedom, but regretting it.

(Do you have any tattoos?)

No and I don't want one, who does?

(Do you celebrate your birthday?)

Birthdays? No, I've never bothered with them.

(Are they ever going to make a movie about you?)

No, I've stopped three Hollywood films to be made over the decades (he had refused to sign the rights away). Unfortunately, in the UK television programs can be made and films without release contracts being signed. I also took legal action to have the three Hollywood films stopped.

I enclosed a classic 'Easy Rider' DVD, the scenes in the cemetery in New Orleans reminded me of my second visit to America and time in New Orleans.

Best wishes

Ian Stewart Brady

which I don't even see!

Mr Kirby Leahey   Ian Stewart-Brady
c. Solicitors
12th Oct 15

Thanks for your letters etc. // Yes, I received the several DVDs you sent, thanks. // However, the "personalised X'mas card" you sent was withheld by Monopoly PCO Trust; second, the cordial Scottish bracelet you sent was also not allowed. I've instructing the Chief Executive Officer to return both prohibited items to you, so let me know when you receive them. You shouldn't bother sending any other items, as all the attention-seeking officials without real jobs here will simply prohibit items to justify their own parasitic existences. Second, it is common knowledge that the more overtly corrupt and criminal the person or system, the more publicly and ostentatiously moral and righteous they must appear to the ignorant. // Brosnan? Never set eyes on him, and never heard of him in 1976! It's common for such people to make empty boasts. // Yes, I'm still bedridden, and now have a chest infection. // As I said, my Frankfurt solicitors and London legal executors will handle my funeral arrangements, and I have been kept informed. // Yes, I'm kept informed of changes to Manchester, not many of them for the better. As with old Glasgow, I prefer the old Manchester. // Glad you took my advice and avoided approaching the gutter media, more worse than ever. In my day people actually went out of their way rather than speak to the media. Quite the opposite these days. As you say, the Andy Warhol prediction that one day everybody would be famous for fifteen minutes; has been surpassed — more like fifteen seconds! // People who become "institutionalised" do so because, consciously or subconsciously, they prefer to be. Brosnan is a prime example of the old lag syndrome; more at home in prison than in the outside world; always talking of freedom but requesting it in reality. // Yes, I have all the movies I need, thanks, and tape cassettes. // No, as I said, I stopped all social events and financially, since 1998, when the Trust to Honour Lifeworths into a regressive violated prison. // Tattoos? I don't, and don't want one! // Birthdays? I never bother with them. // No, I've stopped those attempts to make Hollywood films over the decades.

LETTER FOUR - SEPTEMBER 2016

LETTER FOUR HIGHLIGHTS

September 16, 2016

Dear Cody

Thanks for yours at first and eighth of September and the Laura Biden assassin DVD Denmark Rolled?

Funeral arrangements are all detailed in my will in the hands of my solicitors and London legal executives. There are no sole heirs to my estate.

Enemy of the gate? Yes, I've seen it, it's actually quite a good account of a battle within battle at Stalingrad, but what are my favorite films in general question? As I'm a film buff covering films from the 1920s to the present. There are too many to mention, including UK, US, European and world cinema. Apart from Al Jazeera for real news, I watch documentaries, films, plays and quality series old and new. No reality programs or TV or celebrity trash or spectacles.

So that brings me onto the offer you receive from social media (Cody was contacted from the Jeremy Kyle Show from one of their producers because obviously he was involved in gangs and the criminal fraternity, they wanted him to go on the program to speak to someone who is going down the same route that Cody went down. Cody was to try to help them - he had let Brady know about this offer - which he ended up turning down). These people search the media for targets to appear on such programs as the Jeremy Kyle Show to publicly demonize and ridicule for entertainment of the ignorant rabble. I have trusted contacts in the quality media but never the tabloids or got to television.

(Did you receive my Gobbles and Outlands book?)

Yes, I received the Gobbles and Outlands books, and the pen refills etc. and acknowledged in previous letters to you.

I'm kept well informed by outside sources of all instances of individual exploitation and betrayals of confidence and act accordingly to circumstance or importance by legal and other means. I've had 50 years of experience and some friends don't wait to be asked to be asked to assist by every method.

Try ready Trotsky's 'Crime and Punishment', I've read most of the world's classics. I no longer read much at this late stage. Yes, prison seems to be the only industry left in Liverpool and as I'm the only high-profile prisoner that Ashworth holds to use my name to demonize the mainly chemically embalmed or professional freeloaders stored here and to glorify and justify the overmanned mercy care trust and POA (Mental Prison and its workers) parasite.

I had more freedom and trust in the Durham (The former Prison Brady was in before being transferred to the Hospital Prison) in the 1960s which held the great train-robbers, Mad Frankie Fraser, the Richardsons, the Portland spies etc. where Ronnie Kray and I did the cooking keeping busy and translating books into braille for schools for the blind.

Ashton on the line station (police station that first arrested Brady and Hindley for the murders) we were interrogated by chiefs for 12 hours there in 1965 unsuccessfully. Hyde police headquarters is now empty and disused (this is where the infamous pictures of Brady and Hindley were taken in the hallways of this station)

I enclosed the sign label you requested for Janus (Brady's book).

Best wishes

Ian Stewart Brady

P.S. Early Christmas card enclosed.

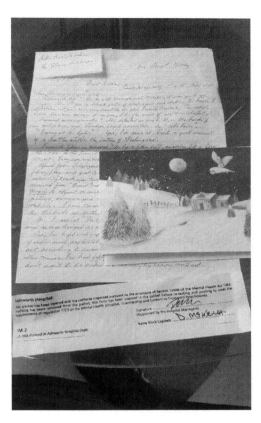

About the Author

Alan R Warren has written several Best-Selling True Crime books and has been one of the hosts and producer of the popular NBC news talk radio show 'House of Mystery' which reviews True Crime, History, Science, Religion, Paranormal Mysteries that we live with every day from a darker, comedic and logical perspective and has interviewed guests such as Robert Kennedy Jr., F. Lee Bailey, Aphrodite Jones, Marcia Clark, Nancy Grace, Dan Abrams and Jesse Ventura. The show is based in Seattle on KKNW 1150 AM and syndicated on the NBC network throughout the United States including on KCAA 106.5 FM Los Angeles/Riverside/Palm Springs, as well in Utah, New Mexico, and Arizona.

Other Books by Alan

Beyond Suspicion: Russell Williams: A Canadian Serial Killer

#1 Bestselling Book in True Crime Depositions

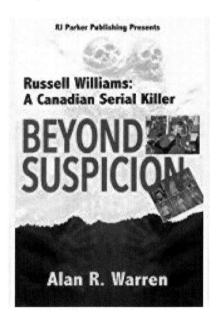

Young girl's panties started to go missing; sexual assaults began to occur, and then female bodies were found! Soon this quiet town of Tweed, Ontario, was in panic. What's even more shocking was when an upstanding resident stood accused of the assaults. This was not just any man, but a pillar of the community; a decorated military pilot who had flown Canadian Forces VIP aircraft for dignitaries such as the Queen of England, Prince Philip, the Governor General and the Prime Minister of Canada.

This is the story of serial killer Russell Williams, the elite pilot of Canada's Air Force One, and the innocent victims he murdered. Unlike other serial killers, Williams seemed very unaffected about his crimes and leading two different lives.

Alan R. Warren describes the secret life including the abductions, rape and murders that were unleashed on an unsuspecting community. Included are letters written to the victims by Williams and descriptions of the assaults and rapes as seen on videos and photos taken by Williams during the attacks.

This updated version also contains the full brilliant police interrogation of Williams and his confession, and the twisted way in which Williams planned to pin his crimes on his unsuspecting neighbor.

Amazon United States
Amazon Canada
Amazon United Kingdom

Deadly Betrayal: The True Story of Jennifer Pan - Daughter from Hell

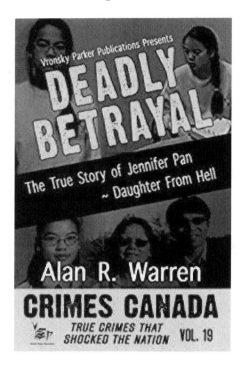

Find out what really happened when seasoned true crime reporter and author, Alan R. Warren, takes you through the details as they unfold in this book of a Deadly Betrayal.

A family of three tied up, each with a gun to their head. "Where's the money? Where's the fucking money?" one of the intruders yelled. A petrified daughter tortured and forced to listen to her parents being shot in cold blood. "I heard shots, like pops," she told the 911 operator, "somebody's broke into our home, please, I need help!" Was this a home invasion? Or something else, more sinister, a Deadly Betrayal.

The real-life horror story that happened inside the Pan family home shocked their normally peaceful upscale Toronto neighborhood. The Pans were an example of an immigrant family. Hann and his wife, Bich Pan, fled from Vietnam to Canada after the U.S.-Vietnamese war to find a better life. Their daughter, Jennifer, was an Olympic-caliber figure skater, an award-winning pianist, and a straight A student.

The Pans worked their way up in this rags-to-riches story, now living in a beautiful home with luxury cars in the driveway. Was it these expensive items that lured three intruders with guns into their home on the night of November 8, 2010?

Amazon United States
Amazon Canada
Amazon United Kingdom

View ALL BOOKS by the Author at:

https://www.amazon.com/Alan-R.-Warren/e/B01LG8S48Y

REFERENCES

1.   https://web.archive.org/web/201306300
31741/http://schadenfreudeuk.blogspot.ca/2011/03/lesle
y-ann-downey-tape-transcript.html

2.   Topping, Peter, Topping – The
Autobiography of the Police Chief in the Moors Murder
Case, Angus & Robertson, London, 1989

3.   Syme, Anthony, Murder on the Moors,
Horwitz Publications, Sydney, 1966

4.   Potter, John Deane, The Monsters of
the Moors, Elek, London, 1966

5.   Keightley, Alan. Ian Brady: The untold
story of the Moors Murders (Kindle Locations 7512-
7513). Pavilion Books. Kindle Edition.

6.   Marchbanks, David, The Moor Murders,
Leslie Frewin, London, 1966

7.   Harrison, Fred, Brady and Hindley –
Genesis of the Moors Murders, Grafton, London, 1987

8.   Goodman, Jonathan, The Moors
Murders: The Trial of Myra Hindley and Ian Brady, David
& Charles, London, 1986

9.   Brady, Ian, The Gates of Janus, Feral
House, Los Angeles, 2001

10.   Keightley, Dr. Alan, Ian Brady: The
Untold Story of the Moors Murders, Robson Books,
Great Britain 2017.

11.   Moors Murders, The Sun, June 28,
2018   -   https://www.thesun.co.uk/news/2197861/ian-
brady-moors-murders-death-myra-hindley/

12.   Moors Murders: A Notorious Couple and
Their Young Prey, NY Times, May 17, 2017 -
https://www.nytimes.com/2017/05/17/world/europe/moor
s-murders-ian-brady-myra-hindley-victims.html

13.   *Moors Murders, Manchester Evening news, Jan. 18, 2019 - https://www.manchestereveningnews.co.uk/all-about/moors-murders*

14.   *Moors Murders: The Victims of Ian Brady and Myra Hindley, Sky News, May 16, 2017 - https://news.sky.com/story/the-moors-murders-the-victims-of-ian-brady-and-myra-hindley-10879310*